CANADA

Hopewell Cape, on the coast of New Brunswick, has the highest tides in the world, with a range of 18 meters (59 feet) between high and low tide. Tidal erosion has severed these bizarrely sculpted rock formations from the main coastline.

Preceding double page:
A highlight in Jasper
National Park: the
Athabasca Falls thunder
through a narrow canyon
with impressive power.

The delta of the Mackenzie
River: a bird's-eye view of
the landscape of rivulets,
lakes and islands.

CANADA

Photography Christian Heeb
Texts Karl-Ludwig Wetzig

BUCHER

Fall moods at Mary Ann Falls in Cape Breton Highlands National Park. The park, with its deciduous forests, upland plateaus and craggy coastline, is the oldest and largest of the Atlantic Provinces and also contains Nova Scotia's highest peaks, 544 meters (1,784 feet) high.

CONTENT

Two highlights in
Banff National Park:
the crystalline glacier lake of
Lake Louise and the luxurious
"Banff Springs Hotel"
(top and right).

Following double page:
French River on
Prince Edward Island.

Characteristic of the south of Saskatchewan province is the vastness of its prairies, here at Val Marie (top). Saskatchewan grows around one-tenth of the world's wheat.

CANADA – VAST LAND

Glacier-covered Mount Garibaldi
(left). – Green Gables House on
Prince Edward Island (center)
was made famous by the novel
"Anne of Green Gables". – Gary
Gott (right) of the Cree Nation.

Ethnic variety in the population is an important element of the Canadian identity.
The country's multicultural "mosaic" forms a
deliberate distinction from the American "melting pot".

When Christopher Columbus, John Cabot and Jacques Cartier first set foot on the American continent, they believed that they had discovered a new world. These days we know that they were mistaken in many respects, and the descendants of the indigenous population, even then long-established, scoff: "Columbus knew neither where he was going nor where he was. And he did it all on other people's money."

The expression "new" is also inaccurate in a geological sense. In the north of the continent, an area of more than five million square kilometers (around 1,930,000 square miles) is composed of ancient rocks belonging to some of the oldest formations in the earth's crust. The last tectonic shift of this gneiss and granite, billions of years old, was 800 million years ago – long before the first living creatures emerged onto the land. Since then, the Canadian Shield has been still. The ice ages scraped away at these rocks without any appreciable effect. When the huge ice masses melted, oceans were created, the "residual puddles" which today remain as the Great Lakes. These are the dimensions we must envisage to imagine the vast expanse of the Canadian land mass.

Canada is the second largest country in the world, but seems to be the world's greatest projection surface for wishes and dreams. The mere mention of a forthcoming visit is enough to induce a misty-

eyed expression and a soft sigh of "Ah, Canada!"

It is almost ironic to realize that the Iroquois word "kanata" which gave the country its name means roughly "huts" or "settlement", whereas in our imagination it conjures up visions of wide uninhabited spaces and dense forests, inhabited in our mind's eye by more beavers, elks, caribou and bears than people. In fact, only 10 percent of Canada's almost ten million square kilometers (about 3,860,000 square miles) of land has any degree of concentrated population. However, when Canadians talk about their country, listeners could easily gain the impression that they live in a kind of dwarf state. Canadians proverbially suffer from a national inferiority complex and uncertainty regarding their own identity. The question of "what makes Canadians distinctive from the rest of the world" elicits the nonplussed response, "Canadians are the only people on earth who can make love in a canoe."

When the world's great powers meet, Canada's appearances are normally refreshingly modest. The country is a member of the G-8 forum of the world's major economies, and actually occupied first place in the annually issued United Nations Human Development Program Index for seven years in succession (1994 – 2000). Although the USA was in sixth place, Canadians perceive this economic and political heavyweight, coupled with the demographic

Left: Anderson River meanders through the Arctic taiga and tundra and joins the Arctic Ocean. – At the Cree Nation's Duck Lake Pow-Wow (top).

and cultural pressure it exerts from the other side of the 8,900-kilo-meter (5,530-mile) border, as so overpowering that a not insignif-icant part of their self-definition is accounted for by disassociating themselves om the USA.

"The United States was primarily founded on the rights of the indi-vidual, Canada's self-image, on the other hand is based on the

At 1/2 Way Ranch near Kleena Kleene in the Chilkotin region of British Columbia. The farm owners proudly display the skin of a puma they have shot. Many of these mountain lions still live in the Rockies.

conviction that the common good could be (and generally is) more important than the rights of the individual", writes Douglas Coup-land, author of "Generation X", who lives in Vancouver. He believes there is a fundamental difference in the way in which the social contract between the two neighboring countries is under-stood, and explains that this dissimilitude dates back to the era when both countries were founded. Canada's transformation from a French colony into a predominantly English-speaking federation actually took place not least due to an influx of combatants from the losing side in the American War of Independence. As loyalists to the throne, they rejected the individualist ideology of the United States and developed an early form of anti-Americanism. "I speak Eng-lish and French, not American. I believe in peacekeeping, not policing, in diversity, not assimilation" are sentiments that still appeared on T-shirts worn by Canadians for Canada Day on July 1, 2000.

Four out of five Canadians live no further than 500 kilometers (about 300 miles) from the border, for more reasons than the cli-mate alone. The pull exerted by the economic force to the south, ten times greater than Canada itself, is immense. As early as 1918, Canada's infant automotive industry was engulfed by the USA, with its iron and steel industry suffering a similar fate. Today 80 percent of all Canada's exports are destined for the USA, and an equal superiority in communication confronts Canadians every day in the media, where four out of five newspapers and the same number of TV stations come directly from the United States. It is thus no wonder that Canadians insist on the differences between

which a powerful separatism developed and still flourishes in Quebec today. On the other hand, the main provinces of Ontario and Quebec span the language barrier to form the country's dominant economic region, in comparison to which other regions regard themselves as peripheral and have developed specifically regional varieties of consciousness based on differing natural features, eco-

the two countries, and that over half of them are in favor of their government adopting an opposing course.

Indeed, two concepts which have likewise developed from the country's own history have led to the fact that society in Canada is noticeably different from that of its southern neighbor. Both of these factors are associated with resisting pressure to conform. One is the regionalism found in the Canadian provinces. Before the Canadian federation was founded, the threat of annexation by the USA had already forced the victorious British in Canada to grant extensive independent rights to the French majority in Lower Canada, from

Life moves at an easy pace in the country. Twig Works Cottage (top) is in the Chilkotin region near Kleena Kleene. – Horse expert and enthusiast Jessica Benisch also lives in this area.

nomic aspects or settlement structures. This is true of the Prairie Provinces and of British Columbia, which is separated from the rest of the country by the Rocky Mountains; similarly, the Maritimes on the Atlantic coast are very proud of their own unique characteristics.

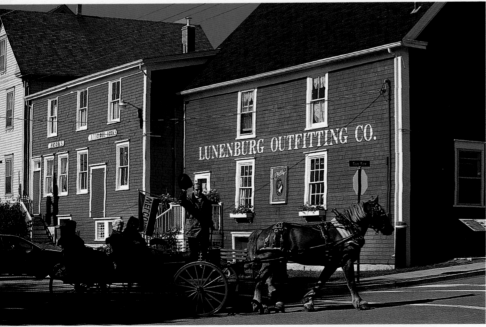

The largest historical monument in the Atlantic Provinces is the reconstructed French fortress of Louisbourg (top). Lunenburg (bottom) was designated a World Heritage Site by UNESCO in 1995.

The other concept, likewise now an official principle of Canadian politics and an idea largely developed on home ground, is multiculturalism. In the 19th century, when the state was subsidizing immigration as a means of colonizing the mid-West, cultural assimilation of immigrants was deliberately abjured, and subsequently, in the mid-1930s, the expression "Canadian mosaic" was coined as a counterpart to America's "melting pot".

In 1963 Prime Minister Pierre Trudeau bridged the diversity in ethnic origin of the Canadian population by stating that Canada was a bilingual but multicultural country in which each ethnic group had the right to maintain and further develop its own culture and values. This principle became law in the 1988 Canadian Multiculturalism Act. Since then the state has been involved in fighting racism and ethnic discrimination, and has promoted a variety of cultural initiatives for ethnic groups such as language courses, newspapers, radio and television stations, libraries and so on, with the aim of allowing national integration to flourish without destroying cultural roots. Given that Canada has experienced few violent tensions or ethnic conflicts in contrast to the USA, this multicultural approach can be said to have been successful, and in any case enjoys widespread support from Canadians, three-quarters of whom view the multicultural nature of the population as an important element of Canadian identity.

"The very same people who tried to take away our identity are now looking for their own," says the Chief of the Kahnawake in Quebec. "I don't have to search for my own identity; I know that I am a Mohawk. But do you know what a Canadian is?" Among young people at least, more and more seem to have the answer. At the last census in 1996, almost 20 percent answered the question about their ethnic origins with the simple answer "Canadian". However, the Chief's confident answer deserves a question mark, since only 30 percent of the First Nations inhabitants gave an indigenous language as their mother tongue; over two-thirds of them learn English or French first.

However, these generous principles of Canadian multiculturalism have appeared comparatively recently in the treatment of the First Nations peoples. As "compensation" for the fact that the government had awarded their land to the white settlers, they were herded into reservations which scarcely afforded them the means to live. Even today, the situation for First Nations peoples living in

see page 20

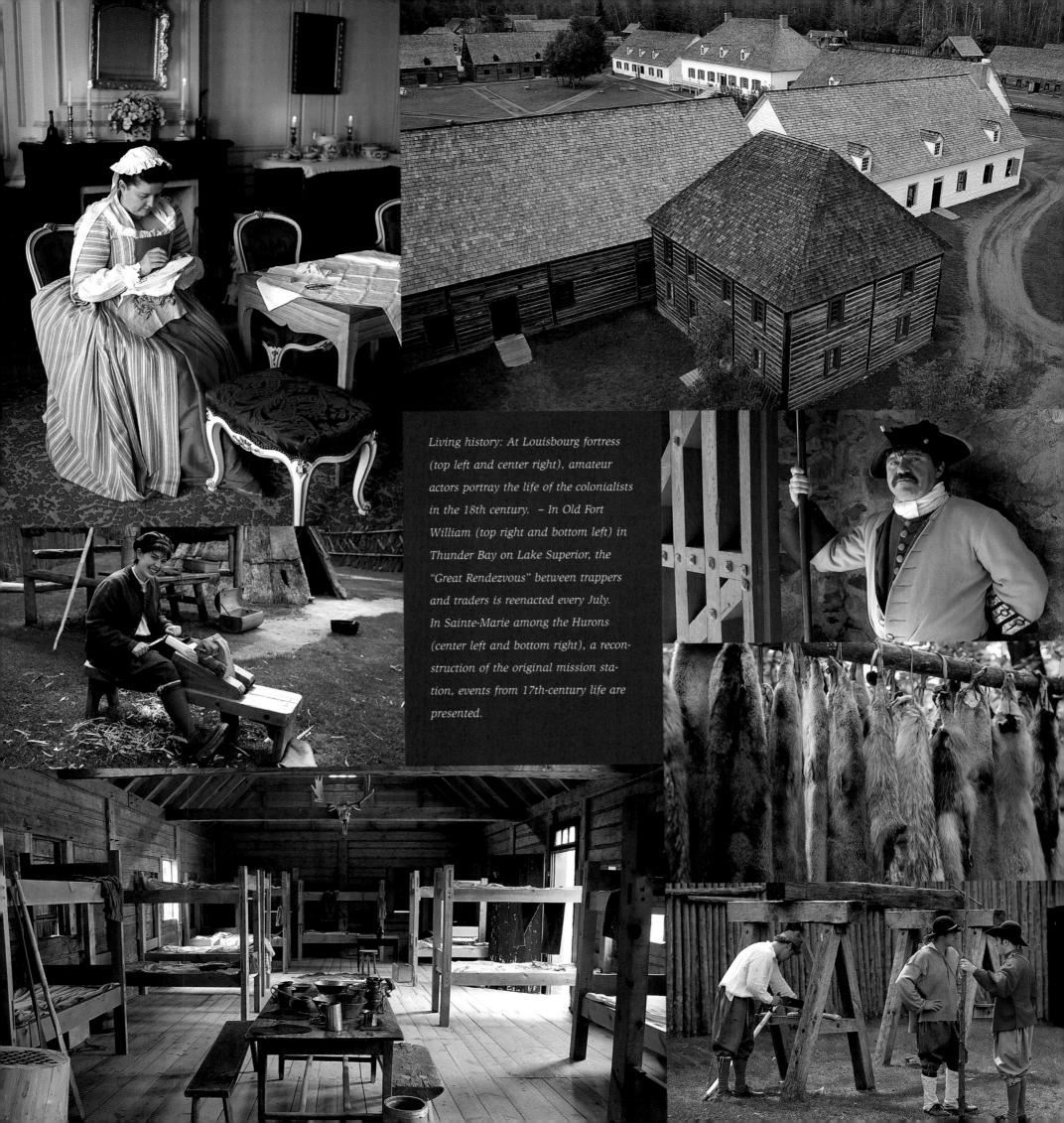

Living history: At Louisbourg fortress (top left and center right), amateur actors portray the life of the colonialists in the 18th century. – In Old Fort William (top right and bottom left) in Thunder Bay on Lake Superior, the "Great Rendezvous" between trappers and traders is reenacted every July. In Sainte-Marie among the Hurons (center left and bottom right), a reconstruction of the original mission station, events from 17th-century life are presented.

THE HISTORY OF CANADA

1605: Samuel de Champlain founded Port Royal, the first European settlement on North American soil; Quebec followed in 1608.

1661: King Louis XIV commanded that every year 300 new settlers should be sent to New

France. By the middle of the 18th century the population had grown to 60,000.

1713: In the Treaty of Utrecht, Newfoundland, Nova Scotia and the area around the Hudson River were ceded to England in return for helping the Bourbons to gain the throne of Spain.

1759: General Wolfe won the Battle of Quebec for England on the Plaines d'Abraham.

1763: Treaty of Paris; France surrendered all but two tiny islands of its North American territories.

1774: The British Parliament passed the Quebec Act, assuring respect for French law and the Catholic religion.

1783: After the United States gained independence, 40,000 loyalist New Englanders streamed over the border into Nova Scotia and Quebec, but were unwilling to join the French feudal system.

1791: With the Constitutional Act, the British government in London separated the old French

colony along the Ottawa River into French-dominated Lower Canada and English-speaking Upper Canada, later the province of Ontario.

1821: The Hudson's Bay Company merged with the North West Company. The flourishing fur trade and increasing demand for timber from the industrialized European countries created a prosperous middle class which demanded greater political self-representation.

1837: Armed uprisings in Montreal and Toronto when London refused to make concessions.

1840: The British Parliament unified Upper and Lower Canada, which were merged into the Province of Canada in the Act of Union in

order to bring the French Canadians under English rule.

1858: Foundation of the new crown colony of British Columbia.

1867: In the British North America Act, »Canada«, Nova Scotia and New Brunswick were unified to form the Dominion of Canada. After the USA had bought Alaska from the Russian Tsar in the same year, in 1869 the London government authorized the British crown to hand over the Rupert's Land of the Hudson's Bay Company to the Canadian state as the Northwest Territories.

1870: The prairie regions were added to the Dominion as the province of Manitoba, fol-

increased between Anglo-Canadians and French Canadians.

1965: The neutral maple leaf replaced the Union Jack as the national symbol.

1976: The separatist Parti Québécois won a three-quarters majority in the Quebec general election, and pressed for preferential treatment for the French. However, in referenda held in 1980 and 1995, Quebec voted to remain in the confederation.

1999: The government and Inuit peoples founded the independent territory of Nunavut.

In recent years, Canada has introduced some of the world's most liberal social policies, for instance the legalization of medical marijuana for the terminally or chronically ill or of gay marriage throughout the country.

In January 2006 parliamentary elections ended 12 years of Liberal rule. In November 2006, Prime Minister Harper succeeded in passing a motion to recognize Quebec as "a nation within a united Canada."

lowed by British Columbia in 1871 and Prince Edward Island in 1873. The Yukon region was awarded territory status in 1898, joined by the provinces of Alberta and Saskatchewan in 1905 and finally by Newfoundland in 1949.

1919: The Dominion, which up to then had not pursued its own foreign policy, was given a seat and a vote in the League of Nations as if an autonomous state. At the Imperial Conferences in 1926, Canada was granted member status with equal rights in the British Commonwealth, and as such declared war on Nazi Germany in September 1939.

1949: Canada became a founding member of NATO. On the domestic front, tensions

Jacques Cartier (1) and Alexander Mackenzie (2). George Vancouver's ships exploring the coast of Burrard Inlet in a painting (1943) by Louis Dodd (3). – European emigrants (photo around 1900) (4). – Opening of the Olympic Games on July 17, 1976 (5).

19

70 meters (230 feet) deep, Capilano Canyon to the northeast of Vancouver can be crossed by the Capilano Suspension Bridge (top). The 140-meter (460-foot) bridge was built in 1899. – Canada's first marine National Park, Pacific Rim National Park on the west coast of Vancouver Island (right), was opened in 1970.

reservations is significantly worse than elsewhere: they receive less education, unemployment is at a constant 30 percent, incomes are so low that most live on the verge of poverty, and suicide among young people is five to eight times higher than the national average. Since the 1960s over 40 percent of Canada's native inhabitants have left the reservations and moved into the cities. Many of them later return at some point and work to improve living conditions on the reservations. They assertively reject foreign expressions such as "Indian", proudly referring to themselves as First Nations.

Even though the way of life on the reservations is still a long way from that of white Canadians, a gradual change in the way people think has been seen. In 1998 the government officially apologized to the First Nations peoples for their former mistreatment, and has finally taken steps to find a solution to the long-delayed issue of land rights. The First Nations are also gradually adopting a more fitting place in Canada's self-image and its history books. "At least 96 percent of our history is the history of the natives before the coming of the Europeans", states a compendium of Canada's First Nations peoples published in 2001. If the history of Canada were represented on a watch face, then the white men would not appear until five minutes to twelve. This as yet final hour did not herald positive times for the First Nations. However, in the future their voices will become more powerful in shaping the destiny of their country.

Dog-power is used by the Inuit
(top), here at Qausuittuq on
Cornwallis Island, to travel over
the ice. – Icebergs in Otto Fjord
at Ellesmere Island (right).

Following double page: The
Dempster Highway runs through
the Canadian Arctic from the
town of Dawson.

Highlights in Nova Scotia:
the picturesque fishing village of
Peggy's Cove (top)
with its lighthouse (right).
The maple leaf, Canada's national
symbol (center). Living history:
Louisbourg fortress (bottom).

ATLANTIC PROVINCES

NEWFOUNDLAND
PRINCE EDWARD ISLAND
NEW BRUNSWICK
QUEBEC
NOVA SCOTIA

Saint John River at Fredericton,
capital of New Brunswick. After
its discovery in 1604 many French
settlers sailed up the river to
settle here as farmers and fishers.

Farm on Prince Edward Island (left).
Quidi Vidi, a fishing village with
characteristic outport houses, in St.
John in Newfoundland (center). –
Farmers proudly display their harvest
of pumpkins (right).

*The small fishing villages and the towns along the Atlantic
with their Loyalist and Acadian influences have retained their charm,
although the inhabitants can no longer make a living from fishing.*

Heavy grey Atlantic rollers, grassy embankments, meadows scattered with bare ridges of rock, patches of heather – perhaps the region appeared so barren to the Europeans as they embarked on their voyage of discovery on the American continent over a thousand years ago.

Around 985, a young Icelander called Bjarni Herjólfsson returned home from a journey to Norway to find that his parents had emigrated to the newly discovered island of Greenland. Without further ado he boarded ship again and set sail to follow them. But fog and wind drove him off course, and when the weather finally improved after many days he saw land which was nothing like the descriptions of Greenland he had been given, with rolling hills and forests instead of mountains or glaciers. Keeping the coast to port, he sailed on and, after two more sightings of land, finally reached Greenland. This masterpiece of navigational skill, accomplished without the aid of a compass, was apparently nothing out of the ordinary for him, as he recounted the story of his discovery only years later when he had returned to Norway.

As a result, the son of Greenland's discoverer Leif Eriksson bought Bjarni's ship and sailed the route he had recounted, but in the opposite direction. He indeed discovered all the regions described, and decided that the southernmost point would be a suitable place to winter, since "there one does not even have to lay in winter fodder for the cattle. At the winter solstice the sun rose at nine and set at three thirty."

In 1960, the Norwegian Helge Ingstad Leifs followed the precise details of the mid-12th-century Icelandic saga recounting the Vikings' exploration of the western edge of the Atlantic, and discovered the place where they had wintered; in L'Anse aux Meadows on the northern tip of Newfoundland, the remains of several buildings dated at around the end of the first millennium were found under the turf, together with other finds which were clearly of Norse origin.

Around the time the "Greenland Saga" was composed, Icelanders would occasionally sail into the Vinland of Bjarni and Leif to replenish the dwindling supplies of timber on their home island. They had discovered that this foreign country was inhabited. At first the natives took to their heels when they heard the bellowing of the Vikings' animals, and later shot at them with arrows from a safe distance; the Vikings thus named them "skroelingjar", cowards, and cut them down at every encounter with their superior iron weapons, which were unknown to the natives. Even this prelude to the encounters with the white men seemed to be the beginning of the end for the First Nations. The Beothuk, for example, a tribe from Newfoundland whom the Native Americans have to thank for the pejorative term "redskins" because of their custom of rubbing red ochre into their faces and bodies, have the tragic distinction of being the first race of people on the North American continent to have been completely eradicated. Nancy Shanawdithit, who died from tuberculosis in 1829 in St. John's,

Left: Balanced Rock at Digby Neck. – Green Gables House (top), built in 1830, was the setting of the novels of Lucy Maud Montgomery (1874–1942).

was the last member of this tribe, which had been constantly persecuted for centuries by the European conquerors. In 1501, the Portuguese sailor Gaspar Corte-Real had dragged off 50 Beothuks as slaves on his first voyage of exploration along the Canadian coast. The Basques were the next to follow the Vikings across the ocean; they had hunted whales on the open seas since the 13th century

"Fall foliage" is the name given by East Canadians to the magnificent colors of the Indian Summer, when the woods and forests adopt their glowing autumnal shades. Here at Grand Falls-Windsor, a town on Newfoundland.

and had crossed the Atlantic in the course of the 15th century, giving the name of Tierra del Labrador to the raw, bleak country on whose coast they dressed their catch and preserved it by drying and salting. Long before Columbus, seamen from Bristol, Hull and other English harbor towns had also "discovered" Vinland anew and named it, somewhat presumptuously, "Newfoundland".

Soon the waters off Newfoundland teemed with Portuguese, Spanish and French ships, attracted by one thing: the legendary wealth of fish on the Grand Bank, where the apparently inexhaustible stocks were systematically depleted using the most sophisticated fishing methods until they finally vanished altogether in 1992. The local fishermen had long been aware of this, and for years the Canadian government tried to introduce quota limits and fishing bans to impose an essential replenishment period for the last great shoals of cod within Canada's fishing grounds. However, outside their boundaries the floating fish factories of the Spanish, French, British and other fishing nations were waiting, using increasingly fine nets to sweep the seabed clean like giant vacuum-cleaners. When the last North Atlantic cod departed from the Canadian coast due to falling water temperatures, the catastrophe was complete. In 1992 the national government in Ottawa was forced to impose a complete fishing ban for over 20 species of fish for an unlimited period. The economy in the maritime provinces of Canada, where the principal source of income was fishing or fish processing, collapsed, and from one day to the next 40,000 people lost their jobs.

result, the majority of the fishermen see no reason to give up their fishing licenses in favor of other sources of income. 14,000 of them await the return of the cod, trying to bridge this waiting period by fishing for lobster. Lobster is therefore easily obtainable at extremely low prices in most restaurants in the Atlantic Provinces, and is also served in simple sandwiches or even on hamburger buns.

The Maritimes have still not recovered from this blow. Although the government supplied billions of Canadian dollars for restructuring and retraining measures, 12 years later life in Newfoundland and Nova Scotia is still seriously affected by unemployment and emigration, especially in the smaller former fishing communities. The catastrophe has turned into an enduring misery. For big investors such as oil magnate Irving from New Brunswick, the vast expanse of Canada offered other places where money could be earned more quickly and more readily, and genuinely large-scale new investments never materialized in the Atlantic coastal provinces. As a

In the rocky north of the island of Cape Breton, part of Nova Scotia, is the Cape Breton Highlands National Park, with light deciduous forests, upland plateaus and a magnificent craggy coastline. The forest trail runs to Lone Shieling, a reconstructed Highland croft.

Glowing fall foliage in New Brunswick: When the mighty maples shed their leaves in October, winter peace comes over the houses of Harvey (top). Herman Dixon, famous as the Pumpkin Man from Riverside, presents the fruits of his labor before they reach the table (right).

Similarly, want had also not infrequently forced the ancestors of today's inhabitants in the Maritime Provinces to leave their homeland on the other shore of the Atlantic. "Lochran àigh nam bochd", the lamp of the poor, was the name given to the moon by the Gaelic-speaking immigrants from the Highlands of Scotland who came to Nova Scotia. Something of the toughness with which they overcame the difficulties and privations in downtrodden Scotland, crossed the sea and built up a new existence in the uncharted Canadian wilderness must have survived amongst their descendants until the present day. In the same way, they retained their love of music which can often ease a heavy burden.

"Grandma used to tell us that at the time when she was newly married all the women washed their clothes in the stream. They would stoke a fire, heat up water in the black pots which they used back then and sing all day long while they were slapping the washing on the stones in perfect rhythm. They believed that the music made the work go more quickly. And the men too would sing as they pulled on the ropes and chains," Alistair MacLeod relates in his Canadian novel "No Great Mischief", about a Scottish clan on Cape Breton Island.

The Maritimes still have a vast store of songs and a strong musical culture today. Anywhere that a few Scottish names are in evidence, the fiddle will not be far away, and even experimental pop musicians like Ashley MacIsaac, highly popular in Nova Scotia, have reinterpreted traditional songs like "Hills of Glenorchy" and "MacDougall's Pride".

Where the St. Andrew's crosses are replaced by French tricolors fluttering from the masts with the yellow star of the Acadians, the people bring out traditional wooden spoons and beat out the rhythms of an old bastringue or gigue between palm and thigh. French folklore in Nova Scotia has at least as venerable a tradition as that of the British. Even before the first English

settlements, the first permanent European settlement on North American soil had been established with the founding of Port Royal by the French, led by Pierre de Monts, in the Bay of Fundy in 1605. A map dated 1548 shows the region as Acadia, an allusion to the

Cape St. Mary's Ecological Reserve is Newfoundland's most fascinating bird reserve. At Bird Rock, hundreds of gannets can be watched against a breathtaking backdrop of cliffs.

Flowerpot Rocks is the name given to Hopewell Rocks in the Bay of Fundy, because of the numerous plants which grow on them. Lichen formations at Northwest River in Terra Nova National Park (bottom).

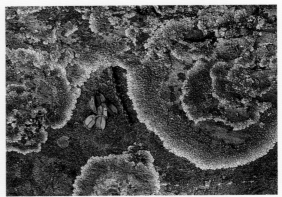

mythical fields of the ancients' paradise. Perhaps it is a reference to the abundance of fish and the enormous numbers of fur-bearing animals; perhaps, though, it is wishful thinking or simply a cunningly chosen name to entice settlers.

They certainly had to work hard for their paradise. The Normans and Bretons who emigrated to Canada were experienced builders of dikes, and they knew how to make simple but effective use of the highest tidal range in the world, draining the reddish alluvial mudflats of the Bay of Fundy and transforming them into fertile marshland where livestock farming, fruit and vegetable gardening are still successfully practiced today. They traded furs peacefully with the indigenous Mi'kmaq and exported their products to Europe. Soon the near-autonomous colony was providing a living for its inhabitants. In 1708, Governor-General Daniel Sgubercase called the Acadians "the happiest people on earth"; however, their great happiness was soon to end.

In 1621, the Scottish-English King James I, paying scant attention to the existing claims of the French, granted all the land between Newfoundland and the New England colony to Scotsman William Alexander. Alexander named the region Nova Scotia and demanded that British colonists emigrate there. In 1710, Great Britain took possession of Port Royal by force and immediately renamed it Annapolis. In the Treaty of Utrecht in 1713, France renounced its claims on Newfoundland, Nova Scotia and Hudson Bay, retaining only the island of Cape Breton. The proud Acadians in the Bay of Fundy refused to swear an oath of allegiance to the British crown and declared themselves neutral. Since at the time the Mi'kmaq were using warlike methods to defend themselves against the ever-increasing tide of British settlers, the English governor initially tolerated this "French neutrality". However, in 1754 the Seven Years' War broke out in Europe and was turned by the British into a world war on the oceans and in the colonies, and Governor Lawrence insisted that the Acadians

See page 45

Unspoilt nature: Cape St. Mary's
Ecological Reserve (top) and
fields of blueberry bushes near
Fundy National Park (right).
Next page: Northwest River.

*Magnificent views:
450-meter (1,475-foot) Perce Rock
(right and top) off the Gaspé Peninsula can be reached on foot at low
tide. The 90-meter (295-foot) cliffs
directly below appear all the more
impressive. The beautiful villa
directly on the sea is bathed in
atmospheric light: Glen Haven in
Nova Scotia (bottom).*

swear their loyalty oath. Once again the Acadians refused. Then began an almost forgotten chapter in America's extensive history of dispossession and banishment. Lawrence ordered that the Acadians be deported and dispersed immediately. More than 7,000 people were shipped off to New England colonies or the British Isles, many dying in the process. Others fled into the forests of the surrounding provinces. But about 10,000 embarked on a long and arduous trek across the continent, following the St. Lawrence, Ohio and Mississippi rivers until they reached the swamplands of Louisiana, still under French rule at the time. There, their descendants, or "Cajuns", a corruption of "Acadians", formed an enclave with its own independent culture, which remained almost unknown until modern times.

At the end of the "French and American War", as the Seven Years' War is known in British history books, the Acadians were granted permission to return to Canada, now wholly under British rule, and some thousands of the displaced came back and settled mainly in Chaleur Bay in New Brunswick and on Cape Breton Island. Today one in three inhabitants of the region is of Acadian stock thanks to their considerably higher birth-rate, which French Canadians gleefully call the "revenge of the cradle". In fact, New Brunswick is the only truly bilingual province in Canada.

Other areas which once served as retreats for the Acadians now include some of the most beautiful natural regions and most popular tourist destinations in eastern Canada. This also applies to the Gaspé Peninsula in the western corner of Quebec, and Cape Breton on the north edge of Nova Scotia. Both regions are closely linked with the sea and are thus typical of Canada's Maritime Provinces. The St. Lawrence River broadens there before Gaspésie into a gulf large enough to swallow the whole of Germany. Here the oxygen-rich Atlantic waters of the cold Labrador Current mingle with the nutrients carried by the numerous rivers and the Great Lakes, and still provide a rich habitat for a wide variety of marine fauna. Thirteen species of whale alone come here for the plentiful food. White belugas spend the whole year in these waters – far south of the waters they usually inhabit. Even in the Saguenay Fjord, which extends

Colorful houses brighten the villages: St-Fabien on Gaspésie (left) and Lunenburg in Nova Scotia (both below).

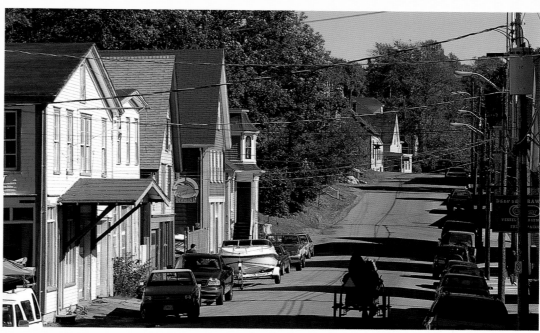

over 100 kilometers (60 miles) into Canada's interior, they can be seen peacefully taking a nap on the surface, resembling distant ice floes.

In Gaspésie itself, the fishing villages are even smaller than in already thinly populated rural Quebec, and both countryside and climate become rougher. The peninsula takes its name from a

A caribou in the fascinating Gros Morne National Park, New-foundland, designated a World Heritage Site by UNESCO (left). West Coast Lighthouse on Prince Edward Island (bottom).

Mi'kmaq word meaning roughly "end of the land"; it is home to the biggest tourist attraction of all, the Rocher Percé, currently 475 meters (about 1,550 feet) in length. At one time there were said to be four arches or openings, but around 150 years ago the penultimate arch crumbled under the pressure of the waves, which continue to gnaw away at the limestone monolith year by year. The bird island of Bonaventure lies further out to sea. 70,000 gannets breed there, circling round and round in the ascending currents and scouring the sea with their keen pale-blue eyes before suddenly plummeting from a height of up to 40 meters

(130 feet), wings furled and powerful beaks outstretched, then plunging through the glassy blue surface of the sea into the depths to seize their prey.

In the south of the Gulf of St. Lawrence, in the unusually warm waters of the Northumberland Strait, lies Prince Edward Island. Although it has been linked to the mainland since 1997 by the longest bridge in the world, the island would like to retain some of the nostalgic rural charm that featured in Lucy Montgomery's popular 19th-century novel "Anne of Green Gables", and succeeds almost effortlessly.

The wind that blows into Nova Scotia, its broad headland jutting out into the open Atlantic, is harsher. It whips the trees behind the hedges and meadow walls into bent, twisted shapes and makes "tuckamore" or stunted trees out of the coniferous forests. Overhead, it often drives white and grey clouds scudding across the broad skies. This is sea country; no point is further than 60 ersaults in the blue sky and a pair of bald eagles circle high above. Three-quarters of the breeding pairs of bald eagles in Nova Scotia have their territory on Cape Breton. "I have travelled around the globe. I have seen the Rockies, the Andes, the Alps and the Highlands of Scotland," wrote the inventor Alexander Graham Bell, "but for sheer beauty, Cape Breton Island beats them all."

kilometers (37 miles) away from the ocean. The Cape Breton Highlands National Park offers the opportunity to experience this open sky from as close a range as possible: high above the meandering, picturesque coast road, the Skyline Trail is a hiking route leading across an extended mountain range to a cape which seems to leap out into the sea. Dense low-growing spruces and balsam firs alternate with grassy clearings, patches of ferns and heather, until the last rocky outcrop is reached, enthroned like an open watchtower over the sea. Great black-backed gulls float below the rock over the sea's silvery mirror, ravens perform som-

The best impression of the diversity of East Canada's landscapes is gained in the region's national parks: grasslands at Lobster Cove in Gros Morne National Park (top), beach at Broad Cove in Cape Breton Highlands National Park (left).

Endless vast and empty landscapes
as far as the eye can see:
on the beach with rocks positioned as
if deliberately arranged (top) or
Broom Point strand in Gros Morne
National Park (right).

Following double page:
The pierced outline of this impressive
rocky outcrop inspired Samuel de
Champlain to name it Rocher Percé
or Perce Rock in 1607.

QUEBEC PROVINCE

FRENCH CANADA

Everywhere in Canada's largest province of Quebec, the normally omnipresent red maple leaf can be seen flying, occasionally at the same height as, but generally below, the royal blue flag with the white fleur-de-lis of the Bourbons. While the majority of the Cana-

dian population speaks English, in Quebec's public image English only appears in the small print at best. The province has its own language law stating that the French language must dominate public statements or announcements, including advertising. All official authorities speak only French, and demand that companies correspond with them in that language. Not until the 1980s, when the English-speaking minority went to the federal courts to claim self-determination as a human right and when a significant number of Anglophones left the country, were some of these language laws repealed.

Such harsh measures are normally a response to grievances and can only be understood by examining their historical background. The phrase "Je me souviens" – I remember – can be found on the license plates of Quebec cars. This historical consciousness aims to maintain awareness of two events: on the one hand, the French were the first Europeans to explore the land, reclaim it and found settlements, and on the other hand, the conquest of French Canada by the British led to permanent subjugation of the French Canadians despite the 1774 Quebec Act.

The comments made by the Earl of Durham in 1838, when he was made Governor of British North America by Queen Victoria, have become infamous. In his report of 1839, he asserted that the "English race", despite their inferior numbers in Lower Canada (Quebec) would predominate over the French in the end "by their superior knowledge, energy, enterprise and wealth". To end their demographic prevalence, he recommended mass immigration and settlement by new colonists from the British Isles and rigorous assimilation of the French Canadians.

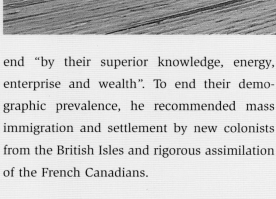

Château Frontenac overlooks Quebec and represents the epitome of the château style of hotel architecture. The Dufferin terrace has a wonderful view of the St. Lawrence River (above). The Place d'Armes (tinted copperplate from 1860, left) has cozy little cafés (far right). The historical ship "The Pelican" in Montreal (right).

Indeed, following this, many English-speaking settlers came to Quebec – particularly the Irish, being Roman Catholic like the French Canadians. Anglophones took the key positions in the economic life of the province; in department stores in Montreal French-speaking customers were served in English only, and francophones commanded lower salaries than English-speakers until 1960 when the politician Jean Lesage demanded, "Il faut que ça change" – this must change. This slogan won the elections for the provincial parliament for Lesage's Parti Libéral and introduced changes known in Canada as the "quiet revolution", comprising limitation of

53

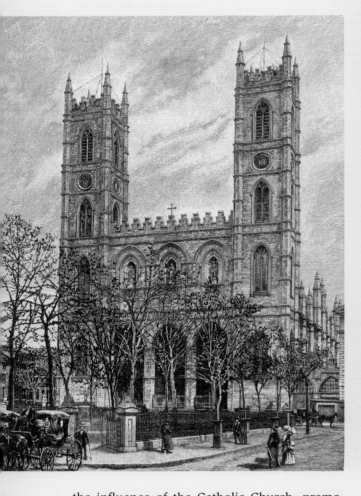

the influence of the Catholic Church, promotion of French Canadian companies and introduction of pro-French language policies. In 1980, voters were asked to decide whether Quebec should withdraw from the Canadian Federation; almost 60 percent voted to stay. In 1995, separatists pressed for another referendum and just failed to reach the necessary majority. The shock hit hard. More than 500 firms transferred their headquarters from Montreal to Toronto.

"We will go on pushing for votes like this until we assemble a majority for independence", is the message from the benches of the Bloc Quebecois, who according to their detractors have gradually turned the referendum into a "nev-erendum"; however, more recently their chances seem to have diminished. Meanwhile, the majority no longer believes that sovereignty has to mean separation from Canada. The indigenous peoples have now joined the debate, pointing out that they had never surrendered their rights to more than 80 percent of the Quebec region to the provincial government, and threatening that if Quebec should actually leave Canada, they could also leave Quebec – together with all the natural resources in their territory. By now, the issue of French roots is losing its relevance, especially with the younger generation who have never experienced discrimination against the French. In the 1996 census, almost twice as many Que-

becois as the national average replied to a question about their ethnic background by stating simply "Canadian". And the number of supporters of independence for Quebec among the inhabitants of Montreal is falling. The metropolis of three million inhabitants is the second-largest French-speaking city in the world after Paris; at the same time, a minority of English native speakers is concentrated in the western districts of the city, but the city is de facto bilingual, as is half of the population of Montreal. When the 165,000 Italians, 54,000 Arabs, 50,000 Greeks, Haitians, Lebanese, Chinese and many other immigrants are included, it is clear that from a multicultural point of view the city is in no way inferior to better-known Toronto. As a result of the French influence, it could be that life in Montreal is actually a little livelier and more fun. In any case the German dramatist and filmdirector Rainer Werner Fassbinder praised it by saying, "Montreal seems to me to be the greatest hope for culture in the western world."

Montreal has a great deal to offer: Notre-Dame Basilica (as pictured in 1884, on the left), Rue de Champlain in Quebec (main picture), the Biosphere displaying the St. Lawrence ecosystem, and the small shops in the old city (top right), the Mount Royal Park above the city (middle right). – Winter fun (photo about 1880, left). The town of Mont Tremblant (below left).

55

Kayak on Whirlpool Lake in Riding Mountain National Park (top). – David Brown builds historic birchbark canoes in Old Ford William (center). Waterfalls in Parc de la Chute Montmorency (bottom).

IN THE COUNTRY OF 10,000 LAKES

QUÉBEC · ONTARIO

MANITOBA

The neo-Gothic buildings on Parliament Hill in Ottawa above the Ottawa River, here forming the border between the provinces of Quebec and Ontario. The Indian word Ottawa means "the place where the waters meet".

By ferry from South Baymouth to Tobermory (left). – Contrasts in Ottawa: the park at the Canadian Museum of Nature (center) and Elgin Street (right).

A region of Canada where nature-lovers can find all they dream of, in this landscape shaped by thousands of lakes, the St. Lawrence River and vast areas of forest.
In addition, Toronto, Montreal, Ottawa and Quebec offer city life in every shape and size.

We are sitting in a small épicier serving top-class French cuisine near the old harbour of Montreal. For the first time in Canada I feel underdressed. My opposite number at this evening meal is fashionably turned out; but after the dignified repast, between the red wine, cheese and coffee, the petite Madame Hébert, so evidently French at first glance with her unruly dark curls, bubbles over: "Quebec is the largest province in Canada, our hydroelectric power stations produce more than half of the country's energy, Quebec is the oldest city in the country recognized by UNESCO as a World Cultural Heritage Site, and the only one in North America which has a city wall, Montreal was the financial center and is on the way to resuming this role, Bombardier is a world-famous company, but when people in Ottawa or Toronto talk of Canada they only think of Ontario. Where does the maple syrup that is the 'glue' of our national identity actually come from? 90 percent of it is from Quebec."

Similar arguments can be heard in other regions too; the Atlantic Provinces, for example, have a total of over 32 seats in the parliament in Ottawa, while Ontario alone has 103 members of parliament (Quebec 75). This imbalance results from the population distribution; over one-third of all Canadians are clustered in the south of Ontario, where over half the country's industrial revenues are also generated.

From the outset, the St. Lawrence River was the primary route into the Canadian landmass, a vital lifeline for the early European

colonies. Since it was extended and made into a seaway in the 1950s, ocean liners have been able to transport goods from industrial centers such as Toronto, Sault Ste. Marie, Thunder Bay, Detroit and Chicago, on the banks of the world's largest lake, without transshipping. No wonder that today this mighty traffic highway is still Canada's "Main Street", along which over half of all Canadians live and where the vast majority of industries and companies have settled. These two aspects are both interdependent and mutually supportive: the urban centers supply infrastructure and workforce, while the universities and research facilities deliver the innovative impetus and the companies offer attractive employment opportunities and financial prospects attracting ever-increasing numbers of people. As a result, Ontario has had a stable influx of immigrants and Canadians from other provinces for decades. Despite the increasing attractiveness of the new growth regions in western Canada, the province attracts more than half of Canada's immigrants year after year.

Many of them find work there in branches of US American companies; when the economic power of the British Empire had begun to stagnate after the First World War, US capital increasingly pressed across the border. To avoid high protection duties, it was cheaper to have the products produced directly in Canadian subsidiaries than to export the goods. As a result, Canadian industries ended up with their backs to the wall or were the subject of takeovers. The auto-

Horseshoe Falls: Canadians are convinced the Canadian side of Niagara Falls (left) is more spectacular than the American side. – Ottawa: sculpture at the parliament building (top).

motive industry is a classic example. In 1905 Ford had already relocated a plant to the other side of the Detroit River in neighboring Windsor, and in 1918 General Motors engulfed its last major Canadian competitors. A similar story took place with the development of the iron and steel industries, and today the dominance of US media giants is almost equally crushing. No wonder that many

Art is also esteemed in Canada: an imaginatively painted fuelling station in Dorion, Ontario (below). – Capturing the atmosphere of downtown Montreal (left).

Canadians are skeptical about attempts to initiate any further merging of both economies into a mutual North American single market. In April 2001, when the heads of governments from the American countries met in Quebec, protected behind barricades 3 meters (10 feet) high, to pave the way for the establishment of a free trade zone for the Americas, globalization opponents from Canada gathered to demonstrate in protest. Against the background of neo-liberal economic doctrine in which corporate market forces were prioritized over national interests, in practice involving the opening of foreign markets to US companies, the

meeting also addressed an explosive bilateral issue: how to grant the USA desert states, particularly California, and Las Vegas access to the water reserves in Canada. According to present forecasts, by 2020 California will have a shortfall in water supplies equal to the amount it consumes today. For this reason the USA has long cast envious glances at Canada, which has the greatest water reserves in the world, and presses for privatization of water supply and distribution. However, an article of the NAFTA treaty states that as soon as companies have started trading water in the USA, the Canadian government may only impose limits in proportion to similar shortages in its own country. Acceptance of a clause like this demonstrates the strength of the economic and political pressure which Canada's enormously powerful neighbor in the south would like to wield.

The hub of economic interdependence is the region known as the "Golden Horseshoe" to the south of Lake Ontario, with Toronto

It is no coincidence that Toronto's actual center has been the finance district since 1966, when the architectural abomination known as the Gardiner Expressway severed it from the waterfront. Here, the skyscraper offices of one bank after another shoot up, an open demonstration of exactly who holds the reins of wealth here in North America's second-largest financial center. The Royal Bank

as its center. The city is a visible symbol of the benefits that Canada can also derive from a close economic relationship with the United States. Until well into the fifties, Toronto lagged far behind Montreal, and was dubbed a "sanctimonious ice-box" by English author Wyndham Lewis since it had more churches than any other city in the British Empire; however, with the coming of the St. Lawrence Seaway it began to grow in importance, and since then has mushroomed with unbroken force. The CN Tower, a compass needle soaring over 500 meters (1,650 feet) above the banks of Lake Ontario, points the direction in which the city is heading: up.

See page 71

Brick houses from the early 19th century fringe the tree-lined avenues in the old quarter of Niagara on the Lake (top). – The basilica of Notre Dame in Ottawa (left).

*Ontario Street in historic Kingston.
Founded in 1673 as a French fur trading post, in 1784 the town became the
Loyalist settlement "King's Town"
(top). – Shopping on a grand scale:
Toronto's Eaton Center (bottom).
The Art Gallery of Ontario, Toronto,
houses the world's largest collection of
statues by Henry Moore, with several of
his "Reclining Figures". The exhibition
rooms were designed by the artist himself (right).*

CULTURE AND NATURE

MUSÉE CANADIEN DES CIVILISATIONS

The view from the capital's Parliament Hill over the Ottawa River, here marking the border between the provinces of Ontario and

The museum is expressly designed to preserve the heritage of all the peoples who have lived in Canada and all the cultures in existence in

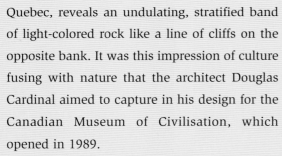

Quebec, reveals an undulating, stratified band of light-colored rock like a line of cliffs on the opposite bank. It was this impression of culture fusing with nature that the architect Douglas Cardinal aimed to capture in his design for the Canadian Museum of Civilisation, which opened in 1989.

Even the museum's exterior is deliberately reminiscent of the land hewn by water, wind and glaciers where the first Canadians arrived at the end of the last Ice Age.

The façade of the museum is composed of slabs of limestone from the prairies which were Canada's most important site of Cretaceous fossils, and fossils can actually be seen in the outer walls.

the country as a collective memory, and to assist in forging a common Canadian identity. Visitors entering from the raised side of the high entrance hall first encounter a panoramic view of the landscape of the Grand Hall, extending over the lower floor to the river below. A full-scale village, with six houses from different tribes and totem poles carved by the natives of the Pacific coast, is set against the backdrop of a Pacific rainforest of red cedars. The glass river façade, providing a magnificent view of the parliament buildings on the other side of the Ottawa River, has moving staircases taking visitors up to Canada Hall. The tour runs from east to west geographically and reviews the last millennium of Canadian his-

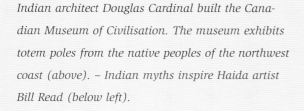

Indian architect Douglas Cardinal built the Canadian Museum of Civilisation. The museum exhibits totem poles from the native peoples of the northwest coast (above). – Indian myths inspire Haida artist Bill Read (below left).

tory, starting at the point where the Viking Leif Eriksson landed in Newfoundland, and continuing through a gloomy passageway representing dark centuries to a 16th-century whaling station. Life-size dioramas portray the hard liv-

ing and working conditions of those times. Scale models and reproductions show the Bay of Fundy, its early settlement and the craft of dike-building brought from France by the Acadians, typical tools and utensils of the French trappers, lumberjacks and loyalist settlers in Upper Canada, and the life of the soldiers in the garrisons along with the hybrid culture of the Métis on the Red River. The next section presents the beginnings of urban civilization, with Victorian shops and characteristic houses from the late 19th century. A coach of the Canadian Pacific Railway gives a view of the grain silos and oil pumps in the prairie. Relax at the end of your tour of the Northwest Territories over refreshments in the "Wildcat Café".

on Front Street clad its reflective windows with 70 kg of gold to create a façade of appropriate pomp; at least it reflects some sunlight into the deep canyons between the post-modern skyscrapers. The streets of Toronto differ pleasantly from those of New York in that they are clean and safe; the crime rate is a mere one-tenth of that in major US cities. These figures are impressive evidence that foreign immigration and multicultural existence need not necessarily lead to an increase in crime. According to statistics from the United Nations, Toronto has the greatest ethnic diversity in the world, with people from almost 170 countries living here and only 17 percent of its population British in origin. The author Michael Ondaatje, an immigrant of Dutch, Tamil and Singhalese extraction, wrote the first great novel about the city ("In the Skin of a Lion", 1987). The concept of multiculturalism, developed in Canada and particularly in Toronto, has played a not insignificant role in the mostly peaceful course of coexistence. In the case of Toronto, an important element for its success has been the outstandingly intelligent city planning since the 1970s throughout the course of renovation and new construction. Deliberate efforts were made to ensure that residential streets and small clearly laid-out districts were preserved among all the offices and business construction. When the offices close, the center does not become a deserted ghost town (like Calgary), and to date no ghettos or slum enclaves have formed, although the gap between Toronto's rich and poor is growing. It is here, and not in the variety of ethnic backgrounds, that future conflicts may be kindled: at present, almost 20 percent of the city's inhabitants already live below the poverty line.

Preceding double page: Montreal by night. – Quebec's old quarter (left-hand page). – Quebec (top) and Place d'Armes in Montreal (bottom).

But if half of all Ontarians will soon be living in the Toronto district and the municipal budget already exceeds that for the whole province of Manitoba, then Canada's largest metropolis is no more Ontario than Ontario is Canada. Countries with vast expanses of open space appear to prefer not to locate their political centers in their major cities: think of Washington, Brasilia or Canberra. Canada is the same; the reason is related to the threat from the United States of America. In the war to conquer Canada, started in 1809 by the fledgling United States, it became clear that both Montreal and Toronto were rendered too vulnerable by their locations.

*The Pacific Railway runs past Nipigon near
Lake Superior (left). – The harbor at
Kingston: The old harbor was built where
the St. Laurence leaves Lake Ontario at the
mouth of the Rideau Canal (bottom).*

Quebec was not acceptable to the Anglo-Canadians, so that in 1857 the question of the capital was presented to Queen Victoria. Examining the map in Buckingham Palace, she pointed to a town of 10,000 people directly on the border between Upper and Lower Canada, a lumberjack town named after a local native tribe and known for its fights and drunkenness – Ottawa. However, when the first elected parliament arrived in Ottawa after the foundation of the Canadian Confederation in 1867, it was able to move into a highly impressive copy of the British Houses of Parliament.

Since then Ottawa has constantly expanded, with "Municipal Improvement Commissions" and city beautification programs. And they bring visible results. At its attractive site on the confluence of the Ottawa, Gatineau and Rideau rivers, Ottawa boasts many public parks, impressive buildings, a host of museums (although the finest, the Musée Canadien des Civilisations, is on Quebec shores in the twin city of Hull), and countless monuments and cenotaphs. However, with 300,000 inhabitants, more than 70,000 of whom are civil servants, it cannot shake off its reputation as "village capital" in the eyes of those from Toronto and Montreal. "The best thing in Ottawa is the train to Montreal", as a former political minister is often quoted as saying.

However, some creatures are drawn to the city. Residents near Ottawa's recreation area of Gatineau Park had to call in gamekeepers over 200 times last year because bears were feasting on the contents of their garbage bins. More than 50 animals had to be transported back to the Laurentian Mountains, and three even had to be shot.

In Canada untamed nature is right on the city's doorstep; and more and more people are adopting leisure pursuits that follow what Canada's most famous author Margaret Atwood once described as the Myth of the North. Atwood wrote that the North, as the "true North, strong and free", enthusiastically heralded in the National Anthem, is deeply engrained in the nation's collective consciousness. However there is no clear geographically definable area bound up with this

The first 55 kilometers (35 miles) of the St. Laurence downstream from Kingston were named Lac des mille îles by the French – although no one has counted them (right).

concept; "north" is simply a compass point, roughly standing for the urge to get away from civilization into unspoilt and largely deserted wilderness.

The lure of the virgin forests in the Indian country of Ontario was so strong that some white people tried to imitate the natives' lifestyle, up to a point where they felt themselves to be Indians.

With a surface area of 82,100 square kilometers (31,700 square miles), Lake Superior – seen here at Montreal River – is the largest of the Great Lakes, and a true inland sea (bottom). – Stone figure at Dyer's Bay on Bruce Peninsula (left).

The most famous of them called himself Wa-sha-quon-asin or Grey Owl of the Ojibwe tribe; his real name was Archibald Belaney, and he came from Hastings in southern England. In 1906, at the age of 17, he left his home for Canada to pursue his dreams of the Wild West. In the forests of Ontario he joined an Ojibwe tribe, married one of the women of the tribe and learnt the art of trapping from her. He later turned to breeding beavers. In an attempt to raise money, he sent a photograph of himself to an English newspaper. Thin-lipped, with a hooked nose and long black (dyed) pigtails, he appeared to be the embodiment of the "noble savage". "Country Life" commissioned him to write a book about his life, making him famous overnight. In 1937 the "redskin" – red in the original sense of the word from dyeing the skin with henna – was received in Buckingham Palace. One year later, Belaney died from the consequences of over-indulgence in alcohol, with which he had deadened his constant fears of exposure. The day after his funeral the "North Bay Nugget" carried the headline: "Grey Owl: English Boy!"

While the revelation robbed an idol of his aura, respect for his good intentions and aims was upheld. Grey Owl was a fraud with noble intent. Beaver Lodge in Prince Albert National Park is still a place of pilgrimage for his readers. For the city-dwellers of the south, a "magic line" ran along the Ottawa River and the northern end of the Niagara escarpment, that distinctive shift in terrain from the Niagara Falls to Manitoulin Island where the bare prehistoric rocks of the Canadian shelf jut northwards from layers of limestone sediment. Today this

tionally proud even by the neighboring indigenous peoples. They view themselves as the protectors of this fragile, barren habitat; in 2002 they secured a landmark contract between nation and nation, awarding them a voice in the proceedings and billions of dollars of compensation, after a 20-year battle with the government over the gigantic power station project in James Bay.

beautiful Canadian region of endless forests and lakes, containing the enormous Algonquin Provincial Park, itself almost 8,000 square kilometers (3,100 square miles) in area, is known as the "Near North Tourist Region".

But for the pioneers and others who opened up Canada, "near" has always been too near. Under contract to major companies and corporations, they have long since set their sights further north to develop the immense ore deposits in the ancient granite and gneiss in the land of the Cree Indians, former nomadic hunters moving between the pine forests and the tundra who are considered excep-

Water landscapes, peaceful and enchanted or vibrant and powerful: at Lake Opeongo in Algonquin Provincial Park (top) and the falls at Kakabeka Falls Provincial Park near Thunder Bay (bottom).

One of Ontario's most remarkable national parks is Bruce Peninsula National Park (both pictures), on the Bruce Trail, Canada's first long-distance hiking trail from Queentown to Tobermory. High above the cliffs or directly at the water's edge, the limestone crags are the perfect vantage-point for a view of Lake Huron.

Following double page: Katherine Cove in Lake Superior Provincial Park.

FUR TRADING
THE HUDSON'S BAY COMPANY

When people in the Northwest Territories speak of The Big Three, they refer to three institutions which still fly the flag in all large towns in Northern Canada today: first, the NWMP (North West Mounted Police), the red-coated policemen who have become part of Canada's national image, secondly the Christian

searching for suitable protective clothing, people discovered that beaver hairs had tiny barbed hooks which could be worked into a type of waterproof felt by milling. While the finished product no longer resembled fur, high society developed a craze for beaver hats, which were even said to have healing properties – they were

Mission, and thirdly The Bay, the local self-service store of the Hudson's Bay Company. Along the Labrador coast, around Hudson's Bay, across the endless tundra in Canada's north up to the islands of the Arctic, the net of the HBC is almost more closely woven than the noteworthy human settlements it serves. A chain of stores as a civilizing force? Indeed, and it is doubly appropriate that the company owed its establishment and rise to a fashion article.

In 17th-century Europe, during the Little Ice Age, the weather deteriorated appreciably. While

said to restore hearing to the deaf, and rubbing beaver oil into the hair was claimed to improve the memory.

No wonder, then, that around 1660 a Boston businessman scented business when two French trappers appeared in the English colony with an enormous load of beaver fur. Médard Chouart and Pierre-Esprit Radisson were the first Europeans to follow the belt of forest to the upper reaches of the Missouri and Mississippi rivers to exchange furs with the native Cree Indians. When they returned, the governor of New

The Hudson's Bay Company held the monopoly in fur trading: The Fur Trade by J. M. Bickell in Edmonton (photo from 1907, left). Fur trader in the far north (photo 1900, middle). An Indian couple exchange furs for a weapon (wood carving, about 1880, from a drawing by C.W. Jeffreys, right top). – At a silver fox trader's for the firm Bredin & Cornwall on Lesser Slave Lake (photo 1904, bottom right). In 1894, the Canadians Dalton and Oulton bred the first wild silver foxes on Prince Edward Island, after stocks in the wild had dwindled.

France confiscated the load and threw the two men into prison for illegal trading. The Boston businessman sailed with them to London and took them to meet Carteret, the First Lord of the Admiralty, who was responsible for the colonies; he introduced them at court.

Prince Rupert, a cousin of the King, became interested in the business and in 1668, invested with royal privileges, sailed into Hudson's Bay in an English ship. The "Eaglet" returned to England the following year with its hold full of beaver pelts.

On May 2, 1670, the Company of Adventurers of England Trading into Hudson's Bay was founded in London. Seventeen private shareholders paid a total of 4,720 pounds sterling for a royal charter awarding an exclusive trading monopoly for all the land whose waters flowed into Hudson's Bay. It would have been impossible for anyone in London at the time to imagine the extent of this area. Rupert's Land, as it was named, covered over four million square kilometers (1.5 million square miles), stretching from the coast of Labrador to the Rocky Mountains and far across today's border with the USA.

A mere 12 years after its foundation, the York factory on the western bank of the Bay brought its owners an annual profit of 200 percent of their original investment. But the two Frenchmen who had started everything once again felt they had been fleeced of their profits, and

founded the Compagnie du Nord in Quebec in 1682. In 1697 a French warship took control of four of the now five English trading posts along Hudson's Bay, although they were returned to the English in 1713 under the terms of the Treaty of Utrecht.

Not until 40 years later did it occur to the British, most of whom stayed in their factories and traded with their Indian fur suppliers through a hatch in the palisade fencing, that the French had not been inactive.

In 1754, one of the expeditions sent into the west by the HBC happened upon some French trappers in what is now Edmonton. Although the French were excluded when French Canada was conquered in 1759, the HBC soon had new competitors.

This time they were mainly Scottish trappers from Montreal who founded their own company in 1784, penetrating far into the west and north by canoe to reach the precious furs before the buyers of the HBC could pre-empt them. Men like David Thompson, Simon Fraser and Alexander Mackenzie – the first white man to reach the Canadian Arctic Sea, in 1789 – undertook their journeys of exploration on behalf of this North West Company, which, in contrast to the HBC, was happy to pay its native suppliers with cheap alcohol.

At the start of the 19th century, skirmishes erupted between the two companies until HBC, under the leadership of financial genius George Simpson, succeeded in taking over NWC in 1821. Throughout a further generation, they defended their territory with all its privilege. Not until 1867, when the colonies merged to form the Dominion of Canada, did a parliamentary committee in London "recommend" that the HBC relinquish their sovereignty to the government in Ottawa owing to the threat of US American annexation in the west. In a generous act (Deed

Snowmobiles park in front of the Hudson's Bay Company branch in Tuktoyaktuk, an Inuit town in the middle of the Canadian Artic in the Northwest Territories. – Painting by Cornelius Krieghoff (1815-1872) "Indians transporting furs through the Canadian wilderness" (oil on canvas, 1858, top center). – A Hudson's Bay Company trading post (picture from 1870, bottom left). – HBC store in Fort Graham and the Hudson's Bay Company in Edmonton (right-hand page, top). – Ships of the Hudson's Bay Company sailed from Gravesend in England to Canada (picture from 1845, right-hand page, center).

of Surrender) in 1870, the still-British HBC sold its quasi-national sovereignty to Canada for 300,000 British pounds, but did not renounce its trade privileges or tax exemptions.

From then on The Bay turned into a busy trading concern. Stores were initially built in the west to supply the two million new settlers in the prairies; at the same time the company became financially involved with the building of the Canadian Pacific Railway. In the First World War, the HBC established a steamship route to supply the Allied forces with Canadian goods,

then opened stores in Paris and New York and became involved with the start of the oil business in Alberta. As a result, it was able to survive the 1929 stock market crash and engulfed other competitors.

Not until 1970, when Queen Elizabeth II signed a further Royal Charter, did the HBC become a Canadian company with headquarters in Winnipeg. 15 years later the HBC was bought up by the Thomson Group and ordered to concentrate mainly on the retail trade. Today The Bay is Canada's largest and oldest department store chain.

*Canadians love their traditions –
here, Cree Indian Bertha Wattunee
at Duck Lake Pow-Wow (top) –
and their Royal Canadian Mounted
Police: Sergeant-Major's Drill in
Regina (bottom). – Pelicans on
Blackstrap Lake (center).*

PRAIRIE
PROVINCES

MANITOBA
SASKATCHEWAN
ALBERTA

Glowing yellow fields of rape
near Edmonton (top).

Calgary Tower (left), 191 meters (627 feet) high. – The church of St. Columba at Moose Jaw (center). Vintage car in Climax, Saskatchewan (right).

The grasslands once roamed by herds of buffalo are now gone.
Today the scene is dominated by vast, rippling fields of corn.
The Great Plains of America.

There has never been a more effective comparison than that of the ocean, even though nowhere on earth except perhaps the steppes of central Asia could be further from the sea than the North American prairies. From the forests of Ontario over 1,400 kilometers (870 miles) of arid, largely flat land stretch ahead, with hardly a tree in sight. This infinity of grass extends through three provinces; each of which is bigger than Ukraine; yet a mere five million or so people live in the three provinces, compared with 50 million in Ukraine (the original home of many immigrants in the Prairie Provinces). Regardless of the direction one looks in the prairie, all there is to see are the tall stems of buffalo grass tickling the sky. A comparison of the prairie and the ocean is more than a mere metaphor: The Manitoba lowlands are actually the floor of an enormous dry glacial sea-bed from the Ice Age, Lake Agassiz; as the millennia progressed, countless layers of sediment settled at the bottom. Harder deposits from the Cretaceous period form its western edge and still appear today as a series of mountain peaks, with the Riding Mountains on the horizon, a clearly visible terrace amid the flat terrain. To the west, behind the Manitoba escarpment rising to a height of over 800 meters (2,600 feet), the prairies of Saskatchewan extend over the plateau. They too were created by the Ice Age, with traces of former sinkholes, glacial lakes and undulating moraine still visible and which have never looked more impressive as grassy "rolling hills" on the big screen than in Kevin Costner's Hollywood epic "Dances with Wolves."

In Elk Island National Park, Edmonton's recreational paradise, elk (top) and bison (left) live side by side with wapiti, beaver and 200 species of bird.

Further west of the Missouri Coteau, a less marked terrace, the prairie rises to heights between 600 and 900 meters (2,000 and 3,000 feet) and even boasts some former nunataks in the shape of the forest-covered Cypress Hills, over 1,400 meters (4,600 feet) high, which once overshadowed the glaciers during the Ice Age. The former meltwater rivers have carved deep chasms in the soft prairie floor and, in south Alberta, have created the craggy badlands; in their scooped and worn rock faces, many dinosaur skeletons buried millions of years ago in the sediment have come to light. All this shows that throughout the course of their history, the prairies have not always had the uniform, flat appearance familiar to us today.

The point where the boreal forest gradually gives way to open parkland in the south once marked the boundary of the natural extent of these grassy steppes, inhabited by rodents and antelope, but also enormous herds of American bison. It has been estimated that around 1830, between 40 and 60 million of these powerful buffalo still lived on the prairies – a rich source of food which naturally did not go unnoticed by the early hunters. One successful hunt would supply a whole tribe with meat for the winter. But before they had horses, how did the hunters approach their prey in this open countryside which afforded no cover?

In 1938, an early hunting-ground was discovered near a Blackfoot reservation where the last foothills of the Rocky Mountains roll into the distance like blue-tinged dunes, and where today dry meadowland fenced in by kilometers of barbed wire alternates with dusty yellow wasteland. Here, for 5,700 years, the hunters of the First Nations had literally forced the buffalo to jump over the cliff at this point. Head-Smashed-In Buffalo Jump is the graphic name of the location, which has been designated a UNESCO World Heritage Site (however, according to the legend the smashed head is not that of a bison, but of a young Indian). It is at exactly the point where the

Every year at the start of July, the famous Calgary Stampede (left) brings the old Wild West alive again – as do the break-neck "chuck wagon races" at the Rockyford Rodeo (bottom).

short grass steppes used to give way to the long grass of the prairie. For the buffalo, this meant a longer supply of food when the winter started. The area is also in the region where the warm winds known as chinooks sweep down from the mountains, also banishing the snow with temperatures of up to 15 degrees Celsius. The hollow of nearby Olsen Creek supplied water for the animals and, as a result, before the winter started, huge herds of buffalo would regularly gather here. By appearing on the edges of the herd, dressed in the skins of wolves and other animals of prey, they were able to drive the buffalo gradually in the direction of a lofty, craggy cliff a good

10 meters (33 feet) high. On the day of the big hunt, beaters would position themselves behind funneled rows of piled stones. They would then light fires behind the herd to make the buffalo panic, the lines of beaters would shout and gesticulate to keep them from running off to the side, and finally the whole herd would stampede wildly over the edge of the cliff into the abyss below.

Until the coming of the white man, dogs were the only beasts of burden kept by the indigenous peoples. When the Siksika, who lived on the Canadian prairies and were known by the white men as Blackfoot, encountered horses for the first time, they called them "elk-dogs".

They probably first "acquired" their own horses from the Snake or Shoshone tribes, whose tribal community also included the Comanche; in the 17th century, these were the first indigenous people to head south where the Spanish were, and steal their horses. The Comanche were soon known as the best riders in the prairies, and to "ride like a Comanche" became an expression of admiration.

herd of bison without using the reins, leaving both hands free for their bows and arrows.

The advent of the horse naturally changed the hunting and living habits of the prairie Indians. A horse always belonged to an individual, not to a whole tribe, so that it became possible for individuals to accumulate personal wealth. The Blackfoot are said to have had the

But the Canadian Blackfoot Indians must also have made forays to procure horses from the Spaniards, adopting from them the Moorish custom of mounting the horse from the right.

In 1754 they were described as an utterly equestrian people by Anthony Henday, the first white man to visit the Blackfoot on commission from the Hudson's Bay Company, and in 1789 as the outstanding equestrian tribe out of all the northern peoples by Alexander Mackenzie. Their expertise with horses was demonstrated particularly clearly by the method they used to train the "buffalo runners", horses which the Blackfoot could steer into the midst of a

Rockyford Rodeo (both pictures): rodeo riding is an exclusively male affair, but after the trials are over, younger fans are allowed to join them. Rodeo disciplines include "saddle bronc", where the rider must stay on the bucking horse as long as possible. A tougher challenge is "bareback bronc" – without the saddle.

Calgary: the City Hall, in rough
sandstone (top) and the city
with Calgary Tower
and skyscrapers (right).
Calgary owes its prosperity to
petroleum; the city is also
famous for holding the largest
Wild West rodeo in the world.

Saskatoon, the modern capital of the province of Saskatchewan, is known as the city of bridges; one spans the South Saskatchewan River (left). Saskatchewan Legislature Building in Regina (below).

greatest stock of horses on the prairie, with up to 300 animals per owner. Their women were also allowed to own horses. A French trapper, Charles Larpenteur, commented in 1860, "It is a wonderful thing to see one of these great members of the Blackfoot tribe with three or four wigwams, five or six wives, twenty to thirty children and fifty to one hundred horses, whose trade turnover can reach two thousand dollars a year."

Once the Indians had horses, they always had the upper hand in combat against an equal number of white men. They were naturally more familiar with the terrain, could move and maneuver extremely flexibly, and by the time the white man had shot and reloaded his muzzle-loader an Indian could already be 100 meters (330 feet) away, or had moved closer and shot twenty arrows. For this reason, the US government south of the border devised the "solution" of unceremoniously depriving the prairie Indians of their livelihood, the bison, in its plans to transform the Great Plains into pasture land for settlers. The construction of the railway was also advanced, to enable hordes of buffalo slaughterers to be transported to the plains. In 1869, the final tracks of the Central Pacific Railway were laid in Utah, completing the first transcontinental railway. Only ten years later, the American bison was facing extinction, the Indians were finally defeated and driven into reservations, and white settlers tilled the land.

The situation in Canada's Prairie Provinces could have developed differently but for a British, or rather Anglo-Canadian, movement of settlers in the last third of the 19th century, which asserted itself – sometimes with violence – against the existing population.

Long before the British arrived, French trappers (coureurs des bois rege) and traders had made contact with the prairie-dwellers. In 1736, the Frenchman La Verendrye was the first to reach the confluence of the Red River and the Assiniboine and set up a small staging-post in the area where Winnipeg would later stand. From that time onward the trappers enjoyed good relations with the prairie tribes. Their alliances with the

See page 99

Transport is essential in the endless prairies: school buses at Edmonton (top) and Calgary freight yard (right). – Following double page: railway lines at Tuxford.

women of the Ojibwe and Cree tribes soon created a new mixed-race population known as Métis or mestizos. However, after the French lost Canada in 1763, the rights to the enormous unexplored regions to the northwest of Quebec and Ontario were transferred to the Hudson's Bay Company, which adopted a kind of "apartheid" policy and strictly rejected this intimacy, or indeed any mixing between the white men and the red men. As a reaction to this, the Métis developed their own unique ethnic self-image: they were French-speakers, although some spoke their own Creole tongue combining French nouns with verbs from the Cree-Algonquin languages known as Michif; they were Catholics and led semi-nomadic lives as hunters and trappers which bore a far greater resemblance to the lives of their Indian relatives than to those of the whites. The intervention of the Métis was largely the reason for the fact that the meeting of whites and First Nations in the Canadian prairies was a far more peaceful process than in the United States. The Métis were particularly expert at making pemmican, a nourishing and long-lasting dried food made of buffalo meat, fat and wild berries for which they had organized an efficient distribution system throughout the whole prairie. Because the Indians also transported furs across the border on their two-wheeled Red River carts, the Hudson's Bay Company viewed this as an infringement of their trading monopoly and implemented penalties against the Métis which only fueled their efforts to achieve separation. The transfer of Rupert's Land to the government in Ottawa, which took place in London in 1869, gave them the opportunity to establish an autonomous region under the leadership of Montreal-educated Louis Riel, with sufficient confidence to embark on negotiations over membership of the fledgling Canadian Confederation. They were supported by the Franco-Canadians in Quebec, who naturally saw a chance of strengthening the French element in the Confederation. When the new Province of Manitoba was established in May 1870, the first Canadian prime minister, John Macdonald, found himself forced to make compromises, accept official bilingual status and allow the Métis to have their own schools. Immediately afterwards, however, Macdonald ordered the army to march into Winnipeg and drive Riel into exile in America. Many Métis left Manitoba and went further west when the government began to press ahead with the construction of the railways, transporting buffalo slaughterers to the American prairies to rob the Métis of their livelihood. In 1885 a last desperate rebellion took

place. The Métis, other groups of prairie Indians who joined the struggle and some white settlers rose up against the government, which sent powerful military forces to Saskatchewan to quash this "Northwest Rebellion". Riel was tried for treason and hanged in

The badlands near Drumheller in the province of Alberta (left and top). A hoodoo at Drumheller. Hoodoos are pillars of earth molded by wind and weather with characteristic "hats" of rock (bottom).

Regina on November 16, 1885. If the Métis had succeeded in asserting their autonomy, an independent Creole culture might have arisen under the broad prairie sky, and Canada's west could have developed into a kind of colorful Brazil of the north.

However, with the abdication of the Hudson's Bay Company, Ottawa's gaze had turned to the prairies. The fur trading companies wanted the

Gigantic combine harvesters are used to harvest the wheat in southern Saskatchewan (left). Vast fields of wheat ripple in the Canadian prairie – Canada's breadbasket (bottom).

distant regions to remain largely uninhabited as hunting reserves for their trappers. The railways enabled the government to chart what had previously been an unimaginably vast area. When demand for Canadian goods increased as a result of the Crimean War in Europe and the USA made further inroads into the northwest after being awarded Oregon (1846), Ottawa tabled a plan of expansionism which called for colonization of the prairies. The experimental settlement launched in 1812 by Scottish Lord Selkirk on the Red River had proved that the prairie soil was fertile enough for agriculture, and so the Métis, the First Nations and the buffalo were forced to cede to the settlers and their livestock. The prairie was divided into square plots of pasture, where succulent Alberta beef has been reared ever since. More land came under the plough, and top quality wheat was found to flourish in the rich brown and black soil. To transport the crops, grain silos were built at regular intervals along the railway tracks, today famous as the enduring landmarks and most significant architectural objects of the Prairie Provinces. The outbreak of the First World War caused demand for Canadian wheat on the world market to soar. At the start of the 1930s Canada was supplying half the world's wheat exports, and remains one of the main suppliers even today.

To accomplish this transformation from natural landscape to arable land, since the advent of the railways Canadian governments have systematically promoted the settlement of immigrants on the prairies. The first to settle were about 7,000 Mennonites from Ukraine, whose expertise in growing wheat on the steppes of southern Russia was to be utilized, and who were actually War Alberta became the richest province in the country. Calgary is Canada's oil metropolis, where more than 400 companies in the oil business have their headquarters. Recently, methods have apparently been developed to exploit the deposits of oil sands which were already known to the white fur traders and First Nations, so that as yet the oil boom shows no signs of abating.

more or less formally recruited. Today there is a steadily increasing flow of immigrants, due solely to the consistently growing amount of employment available in the urban centers of the Prairie Provinces. Alberta in particular has registered three times more immigrants than Ontario and its metropolis of Toronto.
Today, the economy in Alberta is given impetus by the same motor which drives the global economy as a whole: oil. At the outbreak of the First World War in Europe, when the Allies' war machine required enormous volumes of fuel, the first oil field was discovered in Turner Valley south of Calgary. After the end of the Second World

Summer storm over the Trans-Canada Highway, a straight line through the Calgary plains (top). Prairie dog in Grasslands National Park in Saskatchewan. These relations of the squirrel live in burrows and have a yapping cry reminiscent of a barking dog, hence their misleading name (bottom).

Grasslands on the 1,500-meter
(4,920-foot) plateau in Cypress
Hills Provincial Park (top).
Whirlpool Lake in Riding
Mountain National Park
(right). This park has extensive aspen groves.

CYPRESS HILLS

HOLY PLACE OF THE TRIBES FROM THE GREAT PLAINS

Everywhere in the world where people develop a relationship with nature founded in religion, places which are in some way distinctive from their surroundings tend to become regarded as "holy sites". For the tribes on Canada's Great Plains, the Cypress Hills were as significant as the Paha Sapa or the Black Hills were in the spiritual perception of nature of the Prairie Indians south of the border "Me nach tah kak," wonderful hill country, is the name given by the Cree to this low mountain range which, at 1,463 meters (4,800 feet), is the highest point between Labrador and the Rocky Mountains and spans the broad plains of the prairie. Not even the Ice Age glaciers could cover it completely, and so the plateau at its summit 600 meters (around 1,970 feet)

and the Great Plains Indians would set up their winter camps there and embark on a search for visions and spiritual experiences in these lonely mountains.

According to more reliable information than that from New Age shamans or esoteric Indian sources, the first inhabitants of the prairies lived in an inner spiritual connection with the natural world around them, where they believed everything possessed an individual soul. "My grandfather used to tell me about the spirits. They are everywhere in nature … On our expeditions and when we were searching for visions, my people constantly observed the animals, plants, stones, trees, rivers and winds, the sun, the moon, the stars and all things, since our teachings said that the Great

above the plains was spared from being carved with deep canyons by the meltwater rivers when the ice receded. In the winter, buffalo and other game animals would take refuge in the forests on its slopes to find food and shelter from the harsh winds of the open prairie,

Spirit created everything for a reason and purpose. For this reason, we must show respect to everything in nature and learn as much as we can," wrote John Snow, Chief of the Stoneys, in 1977 in his book "These Mountains are our Sacred Places".

Sitting Bull memorial plate in Wood Mountain Regional Park (left). – Sitting Bull and Buffalo Bill (left page, middle). – Sitting Bull (photo around 1885; top). – Conglomerate Cliffs in the Cypress Hills Provincial Park (main picture). – General Custer attacks the Sioux tribes at Little Big Horn (right page, right).

"The Blackfoot believed that whatever they dreamed about would come true," reported James Willard Schultz, a traveling tradesman, who married a Piegan and lived for many years with the Blackfoot in the 1870s.

Crazy Horse, the fearsome war chief of the Oglala who led his tribe to victory in the Battle of the Rosebud in 1876 and who named himself after a dream he had of a wildly galloping horse; was convinced that the world he saw in his dreams was the true world and the other only its shadow and reflection. Many warriors

followed his example and moved out into isolated, deserted spots, hoping through meditation and fasting to experience a vision which would often come in the shape of an animal and which they would henceforth regard as their personal guardian spirit.

For 7,000 years the Cypress Hills were one of the favorite holy places for this kind of spiritual search. When the American Indians lost the battle over the Black Hills despite the victories at Rosebud and Little Big Horn (just before the first centenary of the United States), and Sitting Bull, who had gained a reputation

as a medicine man among the Dakotas, led the last groups of free Plains Indians across the border to Canada in 1877, it was no coincidence that they chose to live in the area of the Cypress Hills.

Two years earlier, Superintendent James Morrow Walsh had established a fort there after an incident with American whiskey smugglers and now, with a section of the newly founded North West Mounted Police – the forerunners of the perennially popular Mounties – he was able to observe the Dakotas until he was transferred due to his undesirably close relations

with them. One year later the Indians were facing starvation and Sitting Bull decided under pressure from Canadian government representatives to return to the United States with his surviving people and to surrender. On July 20, 1881, he handed in his rifle and his horse to the commander of Fort Buford in Montana. "My son has given you my rifle," he said in resignation. "Now he would like to know what he should live from."

After the unconditional surrender and the desolate life in the reservations, many Indians believed that only one way led to hope: a return to the spirits and visions they had once found in their holy mountains, in the Black Hills and Cypress Hills. Around 1890 the Ghost Dance movement was formed, in an attempt to conjure up the fallen warriors from the past.

Spreading like prairie fire, it was quickly outlawed and stamped out by the white authorities. In December 1890 Sitting Bull was shot because a group of ghost dancers had gathered around his hut. Perhaps his spirit returned to the Cypress Hills.

The Duck Lake Pow-Wow in Saskatchewan is a gathering of the Cree where they exchange news and celebrate, donning their finest costumes and headdresses and painting their faces in the traditional manner. The traditional dances are an important ritual.

A seaplane or kayak is needed to explore the Jacobsen Glacier (top) and Bow Lake in Banff National Park (bottom). – A touch of nostalgia in the old gold-rush town of Barkerville (center).

ROCKY MOUN- TAINS

ALBERTA
BRITISH COLUMBIA

*Secluded Maligne Lake, 22 kilo-
meters (14 miles) long and up
to 96 meters (315 feet) deep, fed
by glacier meltwater, is best
explored by boat.*

Hiking all year round: across frozen Lake Louise (left) and on the Berg Lake Trail in Mount Robson Provincial Park (center). Bald eagles (right).

The Rockies belong to some of the most fascinating countryside in Canada: snow-covered peaks, turquoise mountain lakes, four famous national parks, mighty glaciers and a rich diversity of flora and fauna.

We did not believe what our guide had told us, but as we approached they became higher and higher, enormous masses of snow becoming visible through the clouds and forming an impenetrable barrier even for eagles." Thus ran the report of fur trader David Thompson, in 1807 one of the first white men to attempt to cross the Rocky Mountains (and succeeding only some years later after several failures). Since then countless travelers have been transfixed by their first view of the Rockies. "The highest pinnacles of the blackish-grey mountain faces before me are suddenly plunged from above in fiery red, such a glowing red amid the subtle harmony of gentle morning colors that one might imagine the summits had been heated to a dazzling molten glow", enthused German travel writer Alfred E. Johann (1901 to 1996; real name Alfred Ernst Wollschläger) on his approach to these truly "rocky mountains" in contrast to the rolling hills of the prairie.

Like Johann, most visitors take the main approach route to the Rocky Mountains, running from the east through the wheat fields of Saskatchewan and Alberta: the Trans-Canada Highway via Calgary. From there, passing though increasingly hilly foreland and the narrowing valley of the Bow River, they quickly arrive at the best-known and most popular National Parks in the Rockies; Banff and Jasper. However, there is another more scenic approach to the Rockies aside from the main highway – the secondary route over the broad, flat prairie south of Lethbridge to the Waterton Lakes National Park in the very south on the border with Montana. Straight roads with endless fences run through level, corn-gold pastures of dried prairie grass and silver-green sage bushes; each detail, even a simple lilac-painted grain elevator, takes on aesthetic significance in this uniform landscape spanned from horizon to horizon by an infinite sky. Now and then an occasional pickup truck passes, a powerful figure with thick black pigtails at the wheel. We are in the territory of the Blackfoot Indians, who once dominated the region as buffalo hunters, equestrian nomads and fierce warriors. The car radio plays hard rock music alternating with the beating rhythm of Indian drums.

And then they appear, at first seeming to be a mere mirage in the sky, but then indeed looming suddenly out of the plain. The Rocky Mountains. In the Waterton Lakes region, they stand directly on the flat prairie, towering immediately behind the lakes without foothills or forests and crowned with snow-covered peaks 2,500 meters (8,200 feet) high. Golden eagles circle their summits, and below at the entrance to the park a buffalo herd grazes on the plain in the buttery evening light.

The Waterton Lakes National Park, which continues across the border far into the USA as Glacier National Park, is unique in that it encompasses flora and fauna from the flat grasslands, the high uplands of the Rocky Mountains and all the intervening land-

A mother grizzly with her cub, hunting for berries in Banff National Park (left).
The peace at Muncho Lake is particularly spellbinding in the evening (top center).

scapes. It was no coincidence that in 1926 the Canadian Pacific Railway decided to build one of its glamorous railway hotels, the "Prince of Wales", so far from the railway line. Reminiscent of a cross between an oversized Alpine chalet and a Norwegian stave church, it stands enthroned like a cathedral on a natural rocky terrace over the steep banks of the upper lake, the huge windows

Elk in Jasper National Park (left). Floe Lake in Kootenay National Park is surrounded by high mountains. The park, which exceeds 1,400 square kilometers (560 square miles) in area, offers a broadly diverse range of habitats (bottom).

in its hall affording a view over the southern aspect where the lake, the deepest in the Rockies, extends into the high mountains of the Glacier National Park on the American side. Around 900 types of flowering plant and all kinds of wild animals of the Canadian west can be observed here: bison, sousliks, mule deer and coyotes from the prairie, vast numbers of water fowl and beaver on the lakes, white-tailed deer, black bears and elks in the forests, pumas, moose, mountain goats and desert bighorn sheep in higher park regions, and not least a population of nearly 200 grizzly bears, the kings of the Rocky Mountains.

The grizzlies are mainly found on the steep slopes of the Upper Rowe or Lake Cameron, but when the berries in the valley ripen in the late summer they can often be seen in the dense bush next to the road, gobbling and munching their way through the plant kingdom all day long.

Even on all fours their impressive size and strength is apparent. Their typical humps and fur with the silver-grey tips (grizzles) from which their name is derived conceal powerful muscle. No one really wants to risk being threatened by a grizzly rearing up on its back legs, so visitors stay obediently in their cars or, if hiking, wear one of the bear bells available everywhere to avoid surprising "ursus arctos horribilis" by chance and triggering a panic-fuelled attack. Wildlife observers normally move through the forest as quietly as possible in order to watch the animals. Here, however, signs everywhere instruct "Beware! You are in bear country. Make noise, whistle or sing!"

ligerent grizzly fails to be satisfied even when you throw your rucksack full of honeyed muesli bars at his feet, then the rangers advise one last resort: roll into a ball on the ground, cover your head with your arms and endure the attack, in the hope that despite the scratches and bites you might still make it to hospital alive. Perhaps it is better to respect the eccentricities of these

What can happen to anyone who happens to come across a three-meter (10-foot), 500-kilogram (1,100-pound) grizzly is described in all its futility in the ubiquitous information brochures. Running away simply encourages pursuit, and a grizzly can accelerate to the speed of a racehorse in a short distance. In climbing a tree, it is doubtful whether you would be fast enough to evade the claws or whether the bear might not ultimately prove to be the better climber. He would be neither impressed nor discouraged by a dog, but would, if in doubt, simply devour it as a welcome canapé. And if a surprised and bel-

The Yoho is a whitewater mountain river in Yoho National Park. The name of this park, noted for its spectacular scenery, means "awe" in the language of the Cree (top). – Amid magnificent landscapes, Jasper Park Lodge offers holiday comfort in winter and summer. The predecessor of today's lodge was established in the 1920s (left).

Bighorn sheep are nimble climbers and inhabit the mountain forests in Jasper National Park (top). Porcupine (bottom).

bag. It goes without saying that no food should be kept in tents! Although most bears prefer to avoid people, occasional unpleasant encounters can always happen, whether because the bear's natural aggression is triggered by surprise or because the animals recognize humans as easily accessible food (suppliers) after being fed in the past. Recent observations of marked bears in Canada have shown that animals that have attacked humans once are likely to repeat it. Essentially, "problem grizzlies" are not born, but made.

These findings from behavioral researchers are certainly as justified as the safety and behavior advice from the park administration. Yet even so, when drivers on a four-lane highway bordered on each side with wide, cleared strips regularly pass air-conditioned visitor centers with tacky souvenir stands and are confronted by the flashing instruction "Remove sunglasses!" before entering a road tunnel, they may not only be struck by the fact that they are in the heart of the Rocky Mountains in the most popular National Parks of Banff and Jasper: Europeans in particular may be gradually haunted by the unpleasant feeling of being somewhat over-cosseted. After all, they have come from cramped, overpopulated Europe to plunge for once into a virgin wilderness truly deserving of the name, yet just at the point where they would like a little more natural wildness, the Canadians lay asphalt roads in the democratic view that everyone should be able to reach a steep mountain summit with a wonderful panoramic view or the picturesque banks of a lake, even if their physical condition would not normally allow such feats. Mount Revelstoke National Park, for

furry lords of the land and stamp through the forests singing or wearing a jangling bell around your neck like a court jester. The brochures also recommend that after a well-deserved evening barbecue you should change your steak and sausage-scented clothes completely before crawling into your tent and sleeping-

example, features not only a broad asphalted road to enable even the largest motorhome to reach the flat summit. If the last stretch of path (asphalted of course) leading to the observation point is still too much of an effort, visitors can take one of the shuttle buses to the top. At the campsites, the fresh clear water from the

See page 122

116

In the brief weeks of summer, countless species of wild flowers and berries set brilliant accents in the Rockies' many national parks large and small. Botany enthusiasts love the Canadian Rockies, with fireweed and willow rose, pink cat's foot, windflowers, columbine, saxifrage, and mountain avens in addition to many other colorful varieties. The wealth of wild flowers in woods and fields is particularly impressive in the early summer.

Preceding double page:
Peyto Peak Towers tower over the
lake of the same name, so bright
it seems to be straight from a
painter's palette.

Atmospheric Bow River (left)
and popular visitors' destination .
Lake Louise in Banff National
Park (right).

mountain streams is chlorinated, or the faucets carry signs that for safety reasons the water should be boiled – after all, a bear might have … further upstream. The famous Icefields Parkway through Jasper National Park to the Columbia Glacier soon becomes a congested motorway at weekends, and the popular panoramic view of turquoise Lake Peyto, like the untouched

A glimpse into the country coziness of Kootenay Park Lodge (left). Taking the train to Jasper, originally founded as a railway station and midway between East Canada and Vancouver (bottom).

shape of a dog's head amid dense forests, can only be photographed after battling through 15 bu loads of photo-snapping Japanese to mount the observation platform, to say nothing of the hordes of visitors to the breathtaking scenery of Lake Louise. Anyone wanting to enjoy the magnificent views of the giant glacier mountains in their original peace and quiet needs to get up early. This is also true for winter sports fans planning to take the cable car to Canada's largest ski area below the Whitehorn Mountain, where snow is guaranteed for six months of the year from mid-November to mid-May. Spanning a difference in alti-

tude of nearly 1,000 meters (3,280 feet), the area comprises more than 100 different slopes and has its topmost point at over 2,600 meters (around 8,500 feet). Mountain guides were brought in from Switzerland from 1899 to develop accessibility to these wonderful slopes. The enterprising managers of the Canadian Pacific Railway recognized the region's potential for development at an early stage.

As early as 1882, one of their employees was the first white man on Lake Louise, led there by the Stoney Indians. By the following year tracks had been completed from Banff to the lake. At the same time, railway workers William and Thomas McCardell and Frank McCabe discovered hot springs at the foot of Sulphur Mountain in Banff. The railway company reacted immediately: only two years later the chairman, William Cornelius Van Horne, had persuaded the government in Ottawa to found Canada's first National Park at Banff along the lines of Yellowstone National increased the original figure of 100 visitors per season to around 5,000 per year. Extra sections in Tudor style were added to the wooden lodge. However, in 1924 the building burnt down. Within one year – demonstrating the urgency of the desire to recoup financial losses – the railway company replaced it by an enormous eight-storey brick complex. "Chateau Lake Louise"

Park. The railway was responsible for developing the park for tourists.

"Since we cannot export countryside, we have to import visitors," was Van Horne's impish comment. By 1888 the baronial "Banff Springs Hotel" was ready to receive its first guests, followed two years later by the modest one-storey wooden lodge on the banks of Lake Louise, where the National Park now extended. Van Horne defined the lodge as a "hotel for the outdoor adventurer and alpinist". Completion of the Transcontinental Railway, the fastest connection to the Pacific at the time,

Jasper by night (top). – In the late 1800s, hot sulfur springs were discovered in the Rocky Mountains. The Banff Hot Springs Reserve, today Banff National Park, was founded to protect these natural resources. The mineral springs of Cave and Basin Centennial Center are favorites not only with sufferers from gout and rheumatism (left).

Fascinating yet transitory: an ice sculpture at Lake Louise is inspired by Indian symbolism (below). – The deep clefts of Maligne Canyon in Jasper National Park are a paradise for ice climbers (left).

had already become an internationally famous attraction, and from that point the number of visitors grew continuously. Banff, with hardly over 5,000 permanent inhabitants, is located to the south of the park and is the starting-point and supply point for Rocky Mountains holidaymakers in summer and winter alike. While well-heeled more senior tourists are happy to stay in the dignified British-Empire style luxury of the "Banff Springs Hotel" and – naturally at above body temperature – bob up and down in the nearby hot springs, young people and the young at heart cavort in the town at the foot of Sulphur Mountain along Banff Avenue, the plea-sure strip on the opposite bank of Bow River. Skateboard and snowboard shops, fashion outlets, Internet cafés, equipment and souvenir shops thrust themselves for-ward in garish design and blaring music between the Pizza Huts, pubs and steak houses. The perfect mixture for the "fun generation" to hang out and be cool, to dress in the essential hip brands so that at the evening discos and the next day on the slopes they can prove their awareness of what's in and are part of the scene.

These somewhat subjective impressions of the tourism rampant in the Rocky Mountains National Parks are backed up by a few facts. Immediately after the discovery of the hot sulfur springs below Sulphur Mountain while the railway was under construction, the railway company recognized the lucrative potential in marketing the region as a recreational area of beautiful countryside. When the National Parks were founded in 1885, the concept of conservation was pushed well into the background. A far more important aim was to attract an international clientele seeking travel and adventure, and above all with the means to pay for it, in the Canadian Rockies. Conservation was first enforced in the National Park Act of 1930. Exactly 100 years after they were founded, Banff National Park and its three neighboring National Parks of Jasper, Yoho and Kootnay

See page 131

Guests with a taste for adventure can pat huskies or harness a dog team at Wells Gray Guest Ranch, Clearwater.

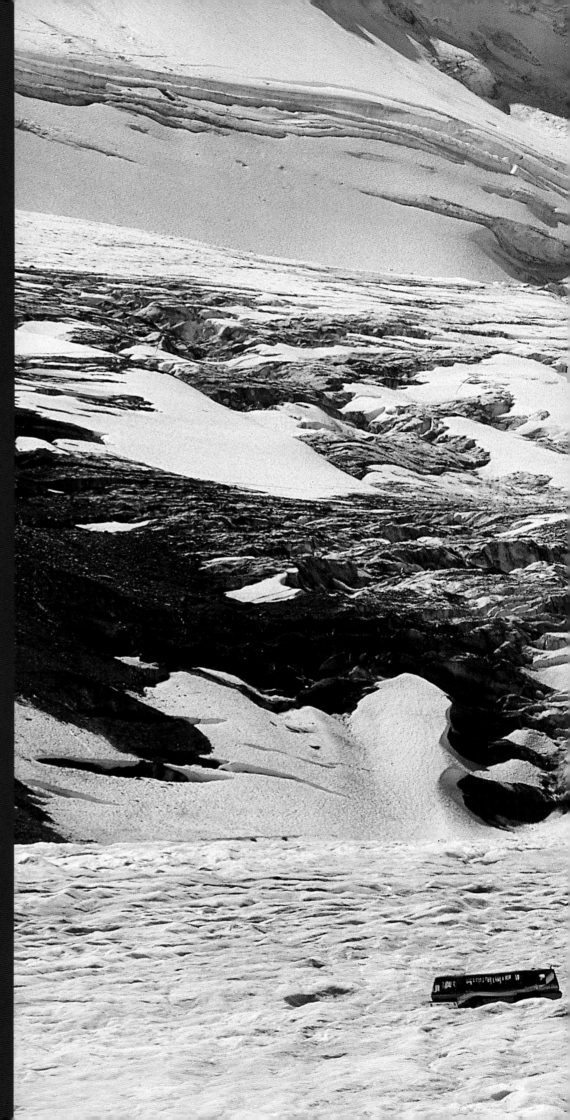

The 230-kilometer (140-mile) Icefields
Parkway, one of the most beautiful
panoramic routes in the world, links
the valleys of the Bow, Mistaya, North
Saskatchewan, Sunwapta and
Athabasca (left). – Columbia Icefield,
the largest continuous ice field in the
Rockies, is traversed by special buses
(right).

Following double page: Maligne
Canyon in Jasper National Park.

Totem poles in Ksan Historical Village (top left) and Kitseguelca (all other pictures). In Ksan young Indian artists can attend a school of carving to learn the traditional art of wood carving at which their ancestors were so adept. The Indians of Canada's northwest coast carved their family crests and family histories in the trunks of cedar trees and erected these picture-covered poles in front of their dwellings. The stylized forms they used represented eagles, ravens, bears or Indian mythical creatures. A great ceremony or potlatch was held in celebration. The Europeans later degraded the significance of these poles to martyrs' stakes.

were awarded the status of World Heritage Sites by UNESCO. Today Canada is divided into 39 different natural regions, based on the idea that each of these natural environments should be preserved in at least one national park. To date, 38 national parks have been opened in 24 of these regions, in addition to provincial parks and small regional protected areas. Canada has reserved a total of 300,000 square kilometers (around 116,000 square miles) for national parks, an area easily covering the size of Italy. The parks attract a total of 15 million visitors every year: of these, some two-thirds, or almost ten million, visit the Rocky Mountains National Parks, even though the parks themselves constitute only 10 percent of the total area of all the parks. Banff alone receives five million visitors each year.

A Pow-Wow is an occasion for the Indians to bring out their gorgeously ornamented costumes and the all-important headdress of feathers and porcupine quills.

Most of these visitors are more than satisfied with the perfectly designed leisure opportunities in the area and the easily accessible main tourist features; otherwise fewer would return. This is good news as far as the natural world is concerned: indeed, it is astonishing that the region has retained so much beauty and diversity of animal life, even around Lake Vermilion on the border directly next to the highway, where beavers, small herds of white-tailed deer and moose and even the odd coyote can be spotted in broad daylight. However, the prospect of all these millions of visitors exploring the unspoilt mountain landscape on their own hardly bears thinking about. It is thus truly a blessing that the crowds stay on the asphalt roads, patiently being driven to Moraine Lake or the huge visitor centers at the foot of the Athabasca Glacier Valley, where they have their

picture taken on the observation terraces against the backdrop of the immense Columbia Ice Fields. This vast sheet of ice, in parts over 360 meters (1,180 feet) deep, flows down from the mountains into three of the world's oceans to the north, west and east: along the Columbia River into the Pacific, down from Athabasca into the Arctic Ocean, and via Saskatchewan into the Hudson Bay and from there into the distant Atlantic. The Columbia Glacier lies precisely on the continental divide and literally forms the high, vaulted roof of North America. Although melting continuously, it still has an impressive area of 300 square kilometers (about 116 square miles); fortunately, this counterbalances the impression of overcrowding at tourist attractions and restores the correct perspective to the true vastness of the Canadian countryside: here all America spreads out at one's feet, with more than enough space to withdraw from other people if required. It is generally adequate to turn off the highway and drive a short way into

All of wood: the work of art at the Visitor Center in New Hazelton (left) and the rustic log cabins built near Anahim Lake (bottom).

the forests – literally, for wherever the tarmac-laying machines or the monstrous felling machines of the lumber companies have not yet penetrated, the landscape is still totally unspoilt and corresponingly impenetrable.

Alternatively, when leaving the central parking area, ignore the signposted route to the observation point and instead follow the next inconspicuous forest track steeply sloping upward, and you will immediately find yourself alone with nature. The arduous climb up to, say, Emerald Lake in Yoho National Park is rewarded with a spellbinding view over its turquoise waters amid moun-

tains gleaming in the red afterglow. This park, with its breathtaking lakes, captivating waterfalls, deep canyons, snow-covered mountains and endless forest, is rightly named Yoho, the Cree expression for "awe and wonder". And when, after two hours of non-stop uphill climbing, we cross the tree line and perhaps meet the first equally solitary hiker on his way down, we manage to gasp out a question about the remaining distance to little Lake Hamilton in its cirque, he glances at his wrist and replies that he's not sure how far, but in any case it's a good 1,000 feet higher. The small glacial lake amid the bare rocky slopes is nowhere near as idyllic as the picture-book beauty below, but on the way, we have enjoyed to the full hours of remoteness in the mountain forests, undisturbed except for our wheezing lungs. Beauty cannot be attained without exertion, whether in art or in nature. As Norman McLean expressed it in his novel "A River Runs Through It", "All beautiful things come from gracefulness,

the cause of earthquakes, volcanoes and lava eruptions, and has compressed igneous magma from the Earth's core between thick layers of Paleozoic sediment to reach heights of almost 4,000 meters (around 13,000 feet) in the case of Mount Robson, and up to 5,959 meters (19,550 feet) in the coastal cordillera of Mount Logan, Canada's highest mountain. The latest findings show that

gracefulness comes from art and art does not come from nothing." It may seem strange to talk of art while face to face with the powerful natural landscapes of the North American continent; however, the colors and forms visible here in the folds of the mountains are probably more reminiscent of the aesthetic principles of a work of art than of the blind forces of nature. And yet at this point, one of the most powerful of those forces was at work: perpetual collisions between the tectonic plates of the Earth's crust along a line of more than 2,000 kilometers (about 1,240 miles) from north to south created long cracks and trenches and formed

A tough job for tough men: Pioneer Log Homes under construction at Anahim Lake in the Chilcotin region of British Columbia. Enormous tree trunks are used to make these coveted wooden houses, which are then delivered to customers in Canada and over the border in the United States (both pictures).

133

ridges and troughs, creasing the deep strata of earth and rock to resemble crumpled paper or tin foil – in fact, numerous mountain silhouettes in the Rocky Mountains bear a resemblance to Frank Gehry's architectural designs. This natural force has been

the earliest uplifting had already begun some 200 million years ago, when the supercontinent of Pangaea broke up and the continents began to move, with the most powerful uplifting taking place in the Mesozoic and Tertiary periods. The Pacific plate is

still moving under the North American plate along the length of the west coast, at the relatively high speed of eight centimeters (3 inches) per year. At the same time, the forces of erosion and climate, wind, rain, frost, ice ages and heatwaves have also been at work for an equal period, scraping, hewing, washing away, eroding and leveling out the high folds of rock. Not only geologists are fascinated by the diversity of structures in the Rocky Mountains created by these natural events.

In 1897, leading German morphologist Albrecht Penck visited the Rocky Mountains and, deeply moved, noted in his report: "A long time we spent there, rapt in the magnificent beauty of the panorama … the almost geometrical regularity in the structure of the layers gave us much food for thought about the complex problem of orogenesis." Often, geological history is visible to the naked eye in the directions of the rock strata. Some, once horizontal, suddenly tilt dramatically at diagonal or even vertical angles; lava can be seen frozen in mid-flow, as can the places where the earth was bent and folded, where it once split and mountains were torn apart or demolished. Like the Alps, the Rocky Mountains are predominantly composed of light limestone and quartzite; interspersed with soft sand and sedimentary rocks, hard granite and gneiss intrusions, lava layers and veins of ore. Depending on the light and the position of the sun, the

Barkerville (all pictures) was the scene where the first nuggets were found in 1862. To commemorate the "Golden Age", a living museum has been established in carefully restored buildings.

mountains can stage a breathtaking show of color and shape, enhanced all the more by the snow caps on the summits, the lakes nestling in hollows and the range of shades and colors of the forests. The beauty and sublimity of this landscape is simply irresistible.

*Enchanted landscapes:
Yellowhead Highway at
Smithers (left), named after the
blond trapper Tête Jaune.
Canoeing, as here on Clearwater Lake (right) in the Chilcotin
region, is the Canadians'
national sport.*

*Following double page:
View in Mount Revelstoke
National Park.*

FROM COAST TO COAST

THE CANADIAN PACIFIC RAILWAY

The mighty project of constructing a railway clear across Canada almost met its doom before construction even got under way, when a financial scandal shook the country. The Conservative government under Mac-

Onderdonk to begin construction of the railway from the Pacific side. The CPR's company history records that Onderdonk preferred "the US method of building a railway: as fast as possible, as cheaply as possible." He bought

Donald awarded the contract to a private consortium headed by Canada's richest businessman, Hugh Allan, who had previously sponsored the Conservatives' election campaign in order to secure the monopoly on coast-to-coast commercial transport. When the scandal broke, the government was forced to resign; the Liberals won the re-election and shelved the project.

Not until the summer of 1875 were the first tracks finally laid for the Canadian Pacific Railway (CPR) at Fort William (Thunder Bay). Two years later, the first train drew into Winnipeg – carried on a freighter. British Columbia sent a warning. To show goodwill, in May 1880 the government ordered US American Andrew

up the labor of 9,000 Chinese immigrants to British Columbia. The arduous and hazardous conditions under which they worked, particularly at the difficult gradient through the valley of the Fraser River in the Canadian Cordillera, is indicated by the number of fatalities. They accounted for 60 percent of all laborers employed, but for almost 90 percent of the 800 deaths during construction. While they dynamited their way through the mountains using nitroglycerine, surveying parties investigated possible routes over the main ridge of the mountains. In 1881/82, Albert Rogers discovered the route over Kicking Horse, 500 meters (1,640 feet) higher, and the pass was subse-

quently named after him as Rogers Pass. For the tracklayers, the steep slope from the west was a nightmare, but the company's new Director General William Van Horne rejected the idea of building tunnels as too time-consuming. The laborers laid tracks up the "Big

The construction of the railway from Winnipeg to the Pacific coast (1879 to 1885) was a masterpiece of engineering, particularly in the stretch crossing the Rockies: shown here, near Field (left). – Bridge over Ottertail Creek (left). – Color lithograph of the Canadian Pacific Railway (top center). – Final section in the Rockies (right). – The Samson locomotive, built 1838, transported coal (far right, bottom).

140

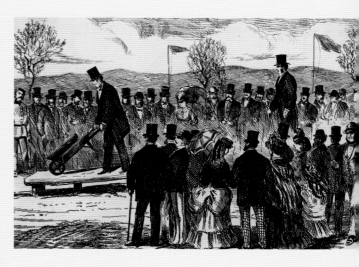

Hill" at an incredible gradient of 4.5 percent. The first train along the route, carrying a number of laborers, plunged into the gorge (not until 1909 was the steep route rendered safer by the construction of two spiral tunnels). The high costs for this and similar sections brought the company to the brink of ruin several times. What was more, in 1883 a conflict with the Blackfoot Indians seemed imminent. An uprising of the Métis at the same time caused the government to subsidize the work by making up the missing capital. When the Métis, led by Louis Riel, rose up a second time in 1885, the CPR used the now completed eastern stretch of railway to rapidly transport 3,000 soldiers to Saskatchewan in order to quell the rebellion. On November 7, 1885, Donald A. Smith hammered in the last rail spike at Craigellachie. The railway enabled the former British colonies of the North American continent to merge into the federation of Canada.

The CPR continued to open up the Rocky Mountains. Railway workers had discovered the hot springs at the foot of Sulphur Mountain, and the company management encouraged the state to buy up the territory around the stopping-point at Banff and establish the first Canadian national park. In 1888 the CPR opened the "Banff Springs Hotel", and in 1894 founded the first "Banff Indian Days", a spectacular folklore event featuring cowboy and Indian games, to which it transported hordes of tourists, "to Kodak the Indians" as the saying went.

141

Tranquil life on Queen Charlotte Islands: orca whales appear off the coast (top), exotic flowers (center) and Bill Ellis in front of his bookstore in Queen Charlotte City (bottom).

PACIFIC
WORLD

BRITISH COLUMBIA

Long Beach on the west coast of
Vancouver Island is part of
Pacific Rim National Park.

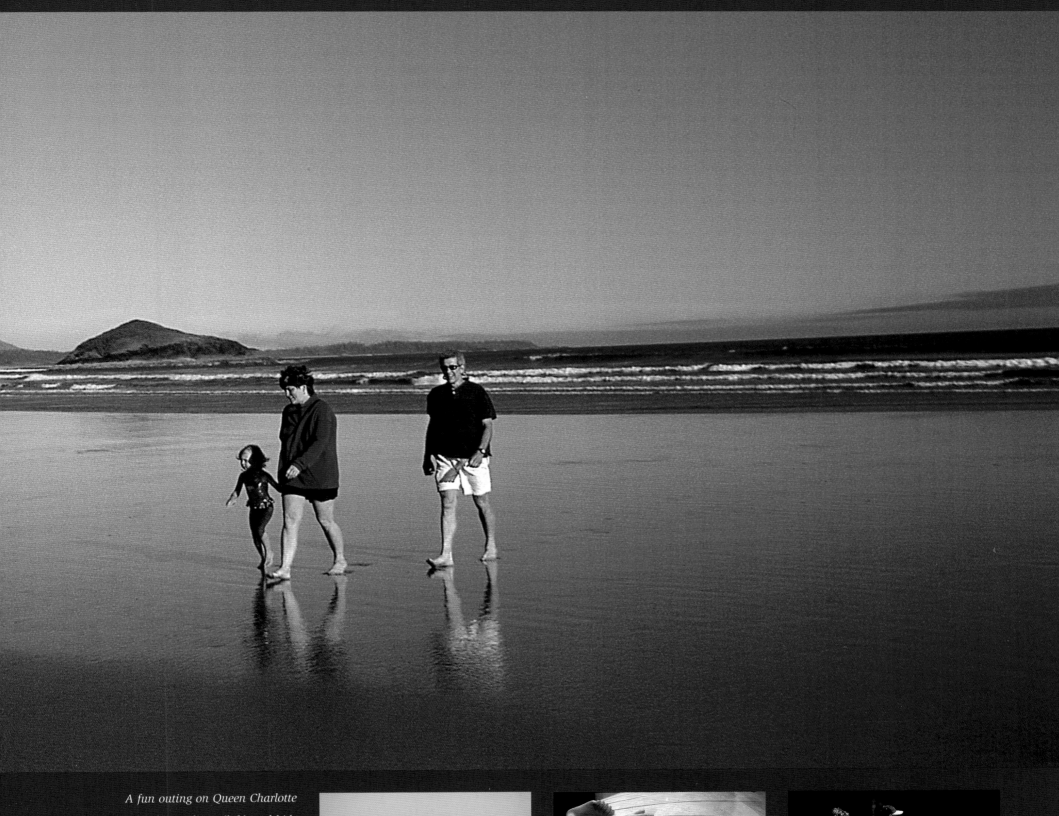

A fun outing on Queen Charlotte
Islands: sea lions (left) and kids
at Sandspit (right). – A sculpture
by Bill Reid illustrating an Indian
creation myth: "The Raven and
the First Man" (center).

Scattered islands, deep fjords, steep cliffs, upland plateaus,
mountain peaks, rainforest, glaciers and even a desert –
British Columbia is the most naturally beautiful province in the country.

In Canada, the abbreviation BC rarely indicates dates from ancient times, but is generally a reference to a province that many believe will be at the forefront of the 21st century: British Columbia. Former US President Bill Clinton agreed with his advisers that this century would be the "Pacific century", and the province of British Columbia, located on the Pacific Ocean, benefited particularly from the boom of the Asian tiger states during the Clinton era. These countries accounted for over one-third of the province's exports, and in return British Columbia accepted the region's immigrants, primarily from Hong Kong. The powerful Asian growth spurt has now begun to falter somewhat, indicated by a slight decline in immigration to BC, but if the trend continues as previously, over one in ten of the province's inhabitants will soon be of Asian origin. Inland flights to Vancouver are easily spotted by the many Asian faces in the check-in lines. The city has one of the largest Chinatowns in North America, which has brought it the name "Hongcouver" for that reason.

Given this definite trend towards favoring the Pacific region, the abbreviation BC is often said to stand for "Beyond Canada"; from its position beyond the gigantic watershed of the Rocky Mountains, BC turns its back on the rest of the country, and is different in many ways from the other provinces – in particular, in its diversity. This applies particularly to its landscape, for the region to the west of the Rockies is geologically no longer part of the Canadian Shield. Here, ancient strata of sediment were crumpled into folds and pierced by new eruptions of volcanic rock. The collision of the Pacific and American tectonic plates not far off the coast created numerous mountain chains, the most easterly of which are the Rocky Mountains. In western British Columbia, a deep fracture zone and an upland plateau lying between mountain ridges gives way to the actual coastal mountains, which in turn give way to a further fracture zone today below sea level, and a further range of cordilleras rising out of the sea as Vancouver Island and the archipelago of Queen Charlotte Islands. These geological events have created a craggy landscape spanning enormous variations in height, which is unique to the whole of Canada.

The collision of the tectonic plates caused – and still causes – enormous subterranean tension, violent upheavals and volcanism. The last volcanic eruption on Canadian territory is said to have occurred around 200 years ago in the Nass Range, BC. However, the danger of major earthquakes is by no means over: quakes up to 9.2 on the Richter scale were last noted in 1946 in the north of Vancouver Island and on the Queen Charlotte Islands. Since that time, a new "big bang" has been expected that could hit the floodplains in the lower reaches of the Fraser River particularly badly – and thus also affect the Greater Vancouver region.

Scattered islands, deep fjords, steep cliffs, upland plateaus overshadowed by lofty mountain crags, dense rainforest, glaciers and even a desert in the very south of Okanagan Valley – this broad diversity of landscape in British Columbia has made Canada's west

A colorful paradise: in 1904, Jenny Butchard laid the foundations for Butchard Gardens, 20 hectares in area, in a quarry belonging to her husband (both pictures).

into a premier tourist attraction. Visitors can be transfixed at the sight of snow-capped peaks of 3,000 meters (around 9,850 feet) in the morning and enjoy the no less impressive sunsets on the coast in the evenings. Tourism has grown into the province's second most important source of income. The province has extensive natural resources; its rich deposits of non-ferrous ores, silver and gold have

Victoria was founded in 1843 when the Hudson's Bay Company moved their head office here and named the new trading post after the British queen then ruling (left and bottom).

been exploited since the whites seized the land. However, British Columbia's greatest treasure is still its "green gold", the wealth of its forests.

This is primarily thanks to the mild Pacific's influence on the harsh climate of the country's interior, bringing westerly winds which carry moist air masses falling as rain on the steep coastal mountains. Up to 8,000 millimeters (315 inches) of rain fall annually on the windward sides of Vancouver Island and the coast. Even Vancouver chalks up over an annual 1,000 liters of precipitation, although snow falls on an average of only twelve days per year. In the

extended vegetation period, this high humidity and moisture caused rainforests to grow in the fertile soils; today they are unique throughout the world. Here, red cedars around 800 years old tower up to 100 meters (330 feet) into the sky, and the tips of hemlock pines and Sitka spruce merge with the low banks of rainclouds that rise mistily over the densely forested slopes.

Two-thirds of the mountain regions of British Columbia were covered in forest when the first sawmills were established in the mid-19th century. The first pulp factories arrived around 1910, and increasing swathes of Canada's forests were sacrificed to the insatiable appetite of its southern neighbor as timber or paper. Over 70 percent of the forests on Vancouver Island vanished when the USA's demand for newsprint soared in the mid-20th century. Even today, 200,000 hectares of forest are felled year after year in the province, almost 90 percent of which are currently still completely cleared by enormous machines – a particularly worrying ecological threat.

And what government is not susceptible to the threat of unemployment? In 1993, the provincial government in Victoria thus announced plans to release 70 percent of the intact, continuous rainforest region at Clayoquot Sound on Vancouver Island for clearfelling. However, the protests of a small action group based in nearby Tofino generated an unexpectedly widespread response,

After such mass clearance, the earth is no longer bound by the tree roots and is eroded by rainfall, causing earth slides that slice vast scars into the landscape.

For a long time, the British Columbian government, which owns almost 95 percent of the province's forests, refrained from taking action on the operations of the major logging companies; after all, exports of their products account for almost half of all exports on the Pacific coast, and total almost twelve billion Canadian dollars per year – an immense sum. In addition, around 15 percent of the inhabitants of British Columbia are employed in the timber industry.

The luxury Empress Hotel in Victoria was built on columns extending 38 meters (125 feet) into the ground of this former swamp (top). – The collection of the Museum of Anthropology (bottom) in Vancouver includes impressive sculptures, carvings and totems.

extending as far as the threat of boycotts from customer countries, and ultimately resulting not only in withdrawal of the "license to cut", but also the first prohibitions of clear-felling and the introduction of legal regulations concerning "forest management", prioritizing the principles of sustainability and biodiversity in forestry. Although the UN declared Clayoquot Sound a biosphere reservation in the year 2000, not until 2002 did the British Columbian government succeed in forging a joint agreement with ecological organizations, the forestry industry and the First Nations over the protection and use of the coastal rainforests.

The history of British Columbia takes on a different aspect from the mere exploitation of its natural resources when the province's indigenous peoples are consulted. They too have always lived, and lived well, from their country's natural resources. Before the coming of the white man, Canada's west was the most highly populated region of the country. The natives also had clearly defined views on ownership rights for natural resources, and even established a society divided into classes of commoners, slaves and hereditary nobility. The culture of the First Nations on the northwest coast was therefore closer to the thinking of the whites than any other in the New World. However, their views on the right to access and utilize natural resources were always complemented by the moral principle of giving, the most spectacular expression of which was the well-known potlatch. (The word is from the Nootka language, and means simply "giving".) The ceremony was basically a means of confirming social events such as the recognition of a new chief, a treaty, a wedding and so on, and of encouraging the chief thus celebrated to reciprocate by bestowing numerous costly gifts from his possessions to the general assembly. In 1884 potlatch ceremonies were prohibited by the white government. Evidently this generous ethic of gift-giving so blatantly contradicted the principles and needs of the economic system of the whites that they felt threatened by it. According to contemporary reports, the government called in troops to use force if necessary to prevent the Indians from participating in their mutual giving and receiving.

The harbor at Vancouver (top). The parliamentary building in Victoria (right) was completed in 1898 by architect Francis Rattenbury.

Giving and receiving must have been the principle by which the first people on this rainforest coast lived 10,000 years ago, after the raven had enticed them from their clamshell. The raven is the great trickster in the mythology of the northwest coastal Indians; always bent on his own pleasure and ready to play unpredictable tricks, he is also an inventive being, perpetually inspired by astonishing new ideas. A creation myth of the Haida people tells of the time before the Great Flood, when the world was still veiled in darkness, blacker than one thousand stormy winter nights; at this time the raven found a house in which the inhabitant had hidden all the light in the universe in a nest of cedarwood chests. The raven changed its shape, gained the trust of the old man and persuaded him to open one chest after another until the final chest revealed the white-hot,

See page 156

VANCOUVER

THE METROPOLIS BETWEEN OCEAN AND MOUNTAINS

Campbell River and Port Alberni on Vancouver Island argue over which has more right to the title of "Salmon Capital of the World", and Vernon in Okanagan Valley is proud to call itself "Fruit Stand Capital of Canada" – why, then should Vancouver not claim the title of "World's Loveliest City?" It may not be evidence of cosmopolitanism, but Canada's largest city can certainly count itself in the Champions League of contenders for the title with regard to its location on the Pacific Ocean. At the foot of the coastal mountains, snow-capped well into early summer, the city center lies on a peninsula washed on three sides by the Fraser River and the Pacific in the Strait of Georgia. This means that only 45 minutes after skiing down Grouse Mountain, it is possible to board a yacht for a sail. From there, the glittering glass and concrete skyline of the two-million-strong city can scarcely be said to blend harmoniously into the beautiful landscape. At the end of the peninsula near the old quarter is Stanley Park, 4 square kilometers (1.5 square miles) in area, with red cedars and Douglas firs hundreds of years old, but also with impressive totem poles from the various bands of the northwest Indians. Governor-General Lord Stanley presented the park to the fledgling city

in 1888, and Vancouver's citizens still delight in their scenic "green lung". Lovers of contrasts will find plenty to attract them in "Hongcouver", not yet 120 years old. The district earned its name well before over 120,000 Chinese emigrated to Vancouver, shortly prior to Hong Kong's return to the People's Republic of China. In fact, thousands had already settled after the city became the final point on the Transcontinental Railway in 1887, a route largely constructed by Chinese laborers. The former Gold Rush hamlet of Gastown and Chinatown are the oldest districts in the city. Although the flow of Asian immigrants has noticeably dwindled since the region suffered economic crisis in recent years, Chinese is now the second language in Vancouver, followed by Punjabi; even German ranks higher than the official national language of French in this colorful melting pot. Over half of all school pupils have a language other than English as their native tongue, so that Vancouver can rival Toronto in multiculturalism; and yet the accentuation is different. Vancouver is a city directed towards the Pacific region, with an atmosphere which has more in common with Seattle, San Francisco or – as German-born author Douglas Coupland, who spends much of his time in

Vancouver, claims – Honolulu, than with the cities in the east of Canada. Vancouver is young, chic, casual and relaxed. Young women making their way to work in the mornings wear jogging trainers with their designer suits. There's always time for a coffee at Starbucks or another of the many coffee shops crowding the downtown streets, before the colorful markets and quays of Granville Island or Kitsilano Beach. "I've never seen so much coffee in my life," said Bette Midler. "The whole city is high on caffeine, yet no-one is rushed."

Vancouver: The Steam Clock (left-hand page, top) emits a cloud of steam on every quarter, whistling in the process. – The statue of a sprinter against the glittering city skyline could almost be a symbol of Vancouver the boom town: for years, the Pacific metropolis has held top ranking as a destination for emigrants (center). – The sailing world anchors before the Royal Yacht Club in Coal Harbour (left-hand page, bottom), with Stanley Park in the background. The 60-meter (200-foot) Lions Gate Bridge has spanned Burrard Fjord since 1938 (left). – Robson Street, the shopping and restaurant paradise, and West Broadway (both top right).

Following double page: The majestic Salmon Glacier near Hyder. Confident drivers can take the tricky Salmon Road across the US border into Alaska.

From the air, the untamed rivers of the Coast Mountains look like veins, meandering endlessly through the wilderness (all pictures).

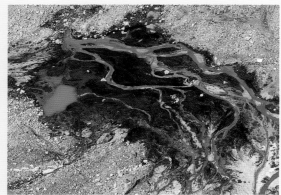

glowing ball of light. The raven quickly took it up in his beak and flew through the smokehole in the ceiling. This was what brought light into the world. However, the world was empty, and the raven was bored. When the Great Flood receded, he hopped along the beach cawing querulously – and, to his surprise, heard a stifled squeaking in reply. Seeking its source, he discovered a great clamshell half-buried in the sand, teeming with tiny creatures which drew back in fear at his mighty shadow. He enticed the small two-legged featherless beings out of the shell to play with them. And so the first humans came into the world, the forefathers of the Haida.

Their home, often wreathed in mysterious mists, was the archipelago of Gwaii Haanas, later renamed Queen Charlotte Islands by the white people in honor of Princess Sophie Charlotte of Mecklenburg-Strelitz, who never set foot there.

The Haida have been suing for years for the return of Gwaii Haanas and the petroleum

156

and natural gas deposits in the sea-bed off its banks.

The raven taught the humans – as the word Haida means – many things, and they learnt to get along in their new environment. In any case the material basis of their uniquely independent culture is believed to be the hunting, fishing and preservation methods they developed between around 5,000 and 3,000 years ago, which enabled them to live richly throughout the year from the then seemingly inexhaustible stocks of Pacific salmon and other fish, and to found permanent settlements on the coast. They used red cedar wood, which was easy to work and did not rot, to build houses of timber shakes up to 120 square meters (about 1,300 square feet) in area, and erected tall poles carved with the totem animals of the families dwelling in the houses. These "totem poles", as the impressive pillars of statuary were known, were later "relocated" to the prairies – where they were never found in reality – by 19th-century popular authors and by Wild West films, and their purpose simply converted; they were described as stakes to

which wrong-doers were bound, and thus re-interpreted, became the primary emblem of all Indians. The cedar forests also supplied the northwest Indians with the material for their canoes, up to 20 meters (65 feet) long and holding 40 men, and for their carvings; they produced masks of high quality, but also designed or richly embellished almost all articles of daily use in a kind of horror vacui.

The crystal-clear water of Little Qualiqum Falls Provincial Park on Vancouver Island (left). Lucky hikers on trekking tours through Queen Charlotte Islands may come across timid roe deer kids (bottom).

Truly impressive exhibits from this advanced culture can be found in the Anthropological Museum in Vancouver – a culture which found all the materials it required for daily culture and art in its natural environment and was able to utilize and work these materials so skillfully that its products were both functional and highly decorative. The peeled bark of the trees felled by the men to build houses and boats was plaited by the women into waterproof baskets and clothing – not unimportant in this rainy coastal region. As the example of the potlatch and the social order show, the Indians of the west coast had not only a highly developed material culture and art, but also an advanced social and spiritual life. Clear evidence of the richness of the indigenous cultures on Canada's Pacific coast is given by their highly distinctive languages. While the dialects spoken by the indigenous peoples on the east coast all belong to the Algonquin family, the west coast has no fewer than eight different language families divided into a host of individual languages and tribal dialects. As shown in the examples above, the Indians preserved a treasure-trove of sagas, legends and mythical tales in the oral tradition of these languages, which provided a framework of explanations of their world, its order and origins. Contemplation of these stories, ideas and traditions was so holy to the Indians that they dedicated an entire season to the procedure. When summer and autumn were over and the process of gathering food and stores for the winter was complete, the season of "tse tsaeka" began, dedicated to sacred things. Dance groups organized into secret societies met in ceremonial houses to dance their traditional knowledge. The

common myths of origin. Only the highest-ranking were accepted into the dance societies and initiated into their secret lore, after weeks as novices and an ascetic initiation period. However, the precise content of this lore is still unknown today, despite intensive research. The Kwakiutl, for example, have a secret society known as Hamatsa after a mythical figure whose name means "Man-Eater at

west coast Indians believed that in the ancient past, mythical animals had given the founding fathers of each clan their own tribal legend, from which the name of the clan, its territory and way of life were derived.

The Nootka, for example, were a Whale tribe, while the Kwakiutl venerated the Dog-salmon; elsewhere there were Seal, Bear and Raven clans. In the sacred season, the members of the secret societies, wearing masks depicting the animal which called each clan into being, a custom which found its pinnacle in the Indians' traditional mask-carving art – danced to remind their fellows of their

Mosses and lichens on Douglas firs and red cedars, making the trees look like enchanted giants. Despite the limited sunshine, many varieties of ferns and berries grow in their protection. Old Grown Rainforest on Queen Charlotte Islands is an ideal place to explore this fascinating world.

Colorful marine beauties: various species
of starfish, jellyfish and crab populate the
coast and the ocean bed. Gwaii Haanas
National Park was opened in 1989 in the
south of Moresby Island, where marine
creatures can be seen in their original
state. These rare animals are best seen
from a canoe or kayak between the 150-
plus islets of the Queen Charlotte archipelago. The misty rainforest oases offer
secluded sandy beaches and are a bird-
watcher's paradise.

the North End of the World". In past times, the legend ran, his followers devoured the flesh of corpses while in a state of ecstasy. Tony Hunt, a Kwakiutl chief and member of Hamatsa, commented laconically, "There's nothing to say about secret societies. They're secret, as their name implies."

The first white men arrived at the territories of these indigenous peoples only later, and they came not from the east, but from the west across the sea. In 1774 it was the Spaniard Juan Perez, and four years later James Cook, on his third and last world voyage. Cook also described in his logbook the great dwelling-houses, heraldic poles and masks, "well designed and executed", which some of the chiefs had worn in "various of their songs". For three weeks the "Resolution" anchored at the northern tip of what would later be named Vancouver Island. During this period trade had developed between the sailors and the natives which, noted Cook, "was pursued by both sides with scrupulous honesty. However, they proved no friends of beads, and also rejected all kinds of clothing." The Pacific First Nations were no primitives; they were fully aware of how trade should be conducted, and were perfectly well able to estimate the value of the goods offered to them in barter.

14 years after these first encounters, an Englishman of Dutch descent returned to these waters as a captain in his own right, after accompanying Cook on his last voyage as well as on his second circumnavigation of the globe from 1772 to 1775. His name was George Vancouver and his mission was to scour the entire coastline from Spanish California to Alaska searching for a channel for the Northwest Passage. Vancouver commenced his task with enormous thoroughness. He set himself three years, regularly wintering in Hawaii, and was finally able to definitively discount any chance of a northwest passage to the south of the Bering Straits. Instead, he discovered other routes including the passage to Queen Charlotte Strait in the Strait of Georgia, proving that the large land mass, which was immediately named after him, was an island. In 1843 the British established Fort Victoria at the southern tip of the island, and in 1849 declared Vancouver Island a crown colony. In 1866 it was assigned to British Columbia and in 1871 entered the Canadian Dominion.

Unlike the east, very few treaties were concluded between the whites and the First Nations during the land seizures by the whites on the west coast, which did not begin until the 19th century. The land rights of the indigenous people were simply ignored by the provincial government until the late 20th century. As late as 1987, the British Columbian Constitutional Court rejected a suit by two First Nations seeking autonomous rule of their land, the Gitskan and

Amazing: first the orca shows its observers the cold shoulder, but then appears to muster them critically. The best place for whale-watching is Gwaii Haanas National Park.

Idyllic water landscapes to relax and recuperate: Hot Springs Island (top), Crescent Inlet (bottom) and canoeing in Insight Passage (right).

first indigenous nation in Canada to seek legal confirmation of their claim to their own land, in 1973. Their claim triggered an avalanche of similar "land claims". Since these claims often involve thousands of square kilometers of land, the court cases are extremely lengthy. In the case of the Nisga'a, an agreement was not reached until 1998: the Indians were awarded over 2,000 square kilometers (around 770 square miles) of land on the lower reaches of the Nass River plus their natural resources, forestry and fishing rights, with ownership to rest with the tribe; here, they were permitted to establish their own administration including a legal system and police force. In return, they waived the traditional freedom from taxation given to reservation Indians. "We are no longer beggars in our own country," said their chief, Joseph Gosnell.

The First Nations had only gradually been reduced to beggars: at first they were regarded as trading partners of equal status to the whites, and their assistance was gladly sought. One man who sought their help was the factor of HBC, James Douglas, who began to build Fort Victoria in 1843. "Spoke to Samose", he wrote in his diary, "and promised him a blanket for every 40 wooden posts they supply, which they were happy to accept." Five days later over 1,200 indigenous Indians turned up for work.

Initially a modest trading office, Victoria was the temporary home of 25,000 gold-hunters in the 1858 Gold Rush, and in 1862 H.M.S. Tynemouth brought over 60 "well-appointed young women" from England to ease the notorious shortage of women in the colony. Upon entry into the Confederation, Victoria became the capital of the newly united province of British Columbia in 1871. Today, it is often mocked as a "city for the newlyweds and nearly-deads". It offers newlyweds the best weather in all of Canada; for its remaining visitors, it is the most thoroughly British city outside London, and anyone with an idea of their own importance can take part in the eminently British ceremony of tea every afternoon at five, in the elegant hotel "The Empress", built in 1908. As a refreshing change from the Americans arriving on pleasure cruises, more and more young Canadians from the east are visiting Victoria to enjoy its wonderful range of outdoor leisure opportunities. Sailors, surfers, divers, kayakers and wilderness hikers form a colorful crowd, meeting up in the many outdoor equipment stores and enjoying the sun in the street cafes between the harbor and Market Square before embarking on their chosen pursuit.

Wet'suet'en, dismissing them with the comment that they were "primitive" cultures with inadequate social organization. And yet the indigenous peoples on the northwest coast in particular had also developed sets of clear regulations governing the rights of ownership and usage of land and natural resources; the Nisga'a in BC were the

Following double page: at Bear Glacier.

RAINFOREST
THE OLDEST TREES IN THE WORLD

When the ancient volcanic island that today is Vancouver Island reared out of the ocean, it was at the geographical latitude of Mexico. The shifting continental plates shunted it into its present position. Yet its impenetrable rainforest appears to have been transported from those very tropics. Dense with moss and strands of lichen. Lumberjacks and timber companies conquered the forest with chainsaws, felling over 70 percent of these woods – believed to be inexhaustible – in the 20th century alone. Industrialists unafraid of taking an axe to the oldest trees in the world are still locked in combat with environmental-

clumps of bracken fern stand over 5 meters (16 feet) high. The entire moisture content evaporating from the Pacific rains down on this rocky, craggy coast in the prevailing westerly winds. Ucluelet, on the windward side of the island, holds the Canadian record for rainfall, at almost 500 millimeters (20 inches) in a single day. The temperate climate and rich soils do the rest: Vancouver Island and the entire coastal region were once covered in rainforest unique in the world, a hermetic green wall of roots, bushes, undergrowth and trees covered ists. Carmanah-Walbran Provincial Park is home to what is probably the world's highest fir, at 96 meters (315 feet) high – already a veritable tree when crusading knights were fighting their way through Europe. Red cedars grow even taller and live longer. One such giant had a trunk fourteen times greater than the armspan of a former lumberjack, now employed by the government to track down trees particularly worthy of protection – making it over 18 meters (59 feet) in diameter. Trees take over 1,000 years to grow to this size. Their dense

The Kermode Bear, here on Princess Royal Island, is a species of white grizzly that has always fascinated humankind. Many legends focus on the "Spirit Bear" (left). – Lichens, ferns and mosses are ideal conditions for the unique fauna, spanning American owls, butterflies and beaver. (right-hand page)

crowns allow only 10 percent of the sunlight to penetrate through to the forest floor, yet this light is enough to bring forth a jungle of lush shade-loving flowers, berries, yew trees,

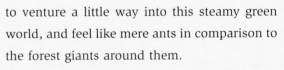

mosses and ferns, with a rich fauna including American mink, red squirrel, deer and black bear. Among the feathered denizens of the woods, the cobalt-blue plumage of the Steller's jays glows especially brightly against their green surroundings.

The provincial government has now established some reservations along the coast of British Columbia to protect particularly valuable remains of this temperate rainforest. In many areas, park rangers have laid out narrow paths and timber trackways enabling visitors to venture a little way into this steamy green world, and feel like mere ants in comparison to the forest giants around them.

The most exciting way to experience the rugged coastline and its lush tangle of hinterland is the West Coast Trail. Well-known to hikers, it was carved through the virgin forest in 1891 as a 77-kilometer (48-mile) telegraph route between Bamfield and Port Renfrew, saving the life of many a shipwrecked sailor on this often stormy coast. Today, the desire to toil through pouring rain along swampy tracks and through deep streams for four to seven days at a time is so popular that ranchers have been forced to introduce a quota system, preventing more than 60 hikers a day from using the impressive trail.

167

*In the Northwest Territories: musk
ox in the Barrenlands (top).
On Pontoon Lake, Ingraham Trail,
Yellowknife (center).
Inuit children in Tuktoyaktuk
(bottom).*

THE HIGH NORTH

NORTHWEST TERRITORIES

YUKON TERRITORY

NUNAVUT

*Ausuittuq (Grise Fjord) on
Ellesmere Island is the most
northerly settlement in Canada,
inhabited by only a few Inuit
families.*

Arctic cottongrass on Baffin Island (left). – Polar bear at Churchill on Hudson Bay (center). Seaplane on Whitefish Lake in the Barrenlands (right).

The northern and Arctic wilderness, including the new province of Nunavut, encompasses 40 percent of Canada's total area. Shaped by ice, the land has few towns and few people.

With glowing hearts we see thee rise, The True North strong and free!" Thus Canada's National Anthem patriotically invokes the True North; yet to stand in the treeless tundra to the north of the 60th latitude that today marks the southern border of the Northwest Territories, buffeted by icy winds that seem to roar straight from the Ice Age of the woolly mammoths, is to confront the end of all idealistic dreams. "One way of viewing a landscape is to recall the methods of dying which are typical of it," muses Margaret Atwood in reference to the True North, imagining in her grim, sardonic style a range of fatalities, from bleeding to death from blackfly bites to hypothermia, which may prematurely end the life of visitors to the True North. The lipless grins of the sailors Torrington, Braine and Hartnell, finally thawed after 138 years asleep in their coffins frozen in solid blocks of ice, also demonstrated that Atwood's imaginings can quickly become deadly reality in Canada's Arctic north. These three were only the first of a total of 130 men who died between 1845 and 1848 during Sir John Franklin's expedition in search of a northwest passage through the icy northern ocean. And they had "only" died of malnourishment and scurvy. Other corpses discovered later bore far more horrific traces. Hunger and acute lead poisoning from the canned food that was the era's new invention had driven them so mad that the remaining survivors, after over two years in the eternal ice, had attacked the others with knives and saws and hacked off

arms or legs as final provender. "At this site, the remainder of the crew, fighting for their lives, had taken the ultimate desperate action," writes Sten Nadolny in his novel about Franklin ("The Discovery of Slowness", 1983) in a delicate euphemism for the act of cannibalism. The tragedy of the ships "HMS Erebus" and "Terror" (what Admiralty cynic would give ships names like that?) was not the only one to mark the search for the Northwest Passage in the True North. Henry Hudson had also been marooned on an ice-floe by his mutinying crew and was never seen again. In 1719, James Knight from the HBC also failed in his endeavor, with two ships.

The "glowing hearts" of the National Anthem are probably necessary in the vast, cold ocean of isolation which is the reality of Canada's high north, when the aim is to attempt to keep reasonably warm and hold onto life in minimum temperatures of minus 63 degrees Celsius. In Resolute, near the magnetic North Pole and the site of the Franklin catastrophe, the season of frost-free days lasts from July 10 to 20 in a good year. It may, however, be shorter.

And so it is all the more impressive that there is a people that has been able to survive for 3,000 years in this desert of ice – albeit suffering great privations in the process. They proudly name themselves Inuit, or "people". Their southerly neighbors, the Cree Indians, called them "raw meat eaters" or Eskimos. This people had adapted so successfully to the often inhumanly harsh conditions in

In Sambaa Deh Falls Territorial Park (left). – A caribou skull in the tundra at Whitefish Lake in the Barrenlands (top).

173

the Arctic that they were able to spread from Siberia around the North Calotte. Even today, the 135,000 Inuit around the world have a common language. The absolute barrenness of their environment forced them to build homes out of frozen water and develop skills and crafts that made movable harpoon heads from the splintered bones of their prey, seaworthy boats from their skin, and artistically

The former Gold Rush town of Dawson with restored, brightly painted houses, in the Yukon Territory (left). At the roulette table in Diamond Tooth Gertie's in Dawson (bottom).

perfected sculptures from their teeth, designed to banish the evil spirits in the natural world. Originally they knew nothing of milk, fruit or vegetables, yet were perfectly healthy before the introduction of Coca-Cola and its ilk. "The secret," revealed Fred Carpenter, born in 1908 as the son of an Inuk woman from Banks Island and an American whaler, "is seal liver. Deep-frozen and eaten raw, it's packed with vitamins."

Speaking of the whalers: during the 19th century more and more came to the waters of the Canadian Arctic in the hunt for blubber, fish oil and the material used in the corsets of fine ladies in Europe and America. On Herschel Island, at the delta of the Mackenzie River, a US American base was founded and used annually as a winter mooring; around 1890, often 15 ships with up to 1,000 crew were trapped in the ice. Encounters with the Inuit became more frequent, bringing them products of civilization such as tobacco and sugar, but also illnesses previously unknown to them. The inhabitants of Baffin Island soon began to refer to Saturday as Sivatarvik, "the day when cookies are distributed". Soon missionaries also arrived, particularly those of the Anglican and Catholic churches, introducing a translation of the Bible into the Inuit's own realm of ideas and developing a syllabary for Inuktituk.

In the north, the modern age of the 20th century appropriately moved in only with the Cold War, when the USA and NATO decided that an early warning system of radar networks, known as the DEW

own First Nations like colonized peoples. In 1960 the Eskimos officially received "the right to consume alcohol" – with corresponding consequences.

"For years, we ignored them. After the Second World War, we then suddenly swamped them with 'welfare'. By doing so, we almost buried their pride," says a government staff member in Aklavik.

(Distant Early Warning) Line, should be set up across the Bering Strait and the Pole as a means of countering the Soviet threat. Soldiers, building teams and the whole retinue required to cater for them set up camps all over the bush and the bare tundra, which were supplied by air. In addition to essential items, they imported enormous quantities of alcohol, the "curse of the North".

In the 1950s and 60s, when Canada supported national independence efforts all over the world as part of the UN, the Ottawa government slowly realized that it could no longer continue to treat its

Just like old times: can-can dancers perform at Diamond Tooth Gertie's (top and left). This "institution" in the far north was Canada's first casino, a legendary dancehall with gaming tables offering not only roulette, blackjack and poker, but also can-can and music.

See Page 182

In Bonfire at Ecoventures Basecamp (both top pictures) at Whitefish Lake in the Barrenlands, life is simple and hearty, both in the cabins and around the campfire. – Breathtaking Northern Lights flicker across the night sky in the Barrenlands of the Northwest Territories (right).

Following double page: An Inuk with his dog team on the southeast coast of Baffin Island.

THE GOLD RUSH
YUKON AND KLONDIKE

In the fall of 1897, over 2,000 people started out from Edmonton, sailing north along the Athabasca, across Great Slave Lake to the Mackenzie River and battling up Liard River or the Nahanni from Fort Simpson – a voyage of 2,500

in his pan than he had ever seen before. The news of his find spread like wildfire as far away as Seattle and San Francisco. The fastest to react took a steamer to Skagway and marched onward on foot, despite the outbreak of winter,

kilometers (1,550 miles) through rain, snow and biting cold. In the first winter, not one reached his destination. At the same time, almost 10,000 were traveling north on a route along Alaska's fjorded coastline, bound for a little river with the Indian name of Throndiuck (Klondike).

In 1895, the Nova Scotia-born gold prospector Robert Henderson had made his first attempts at panning gold in one of the Klondike's many streams and found more gold dust and nuggets over the Chilkoot or the White Pass. Many were not even equipped for winter, and were forced to turn back or froze to death in mountain snowstorms. To call a halt to these senseless deaths, in February 1898 the Canadian government set up a control post at Chilkoot Pass at which anyone intending to pass on the way to the Klondike was obliged to show a year's supply of provisions. Since mules could not tackle the pass, soon an endless line of people formed day after day, dragging their

baggage up the pass. Many needed a good three months and traveled over 2,000 kilometers (1,250 miles) before they had brought their supplies to Lake Bennett, only 50 kilome-

saloon owners and prostitutes settled and founded Dawson City, the most tumultuous gold mining town in America. The quantity of gold mined in the Klondike mountains and brought to

ters (30 miles) away. There they chopped down the forest trees to build rafts on which they sailed down the Yukon. The most hazardous section was at White Horse Rapids, where many of the inexperienced prospectors foundered and drowned until a few enterprising men laid down an 8-kilometer (5-mile) horse track to bypass the gorge. At its end, a settlement rapidly sprang up which was named Whitehorse after the rapids. At the point where the Klondike joined the Yukon, businesspeople,

Dawson increased one hundredfold by the turn of the century. Then, however, the yield plummeted. The gold prospectors vanished even before the first mining companies brought in their diggers in 1904.

Dancer, huts and tents in the gold mining town of Dawson (left-hand page). – Gold prospectors at Chilkoot Pass (center). – Steamer with gold-panning machinery (photo from 1898; top left). – Gold panner at Saskatchewan River, around 1890 (top right).

The Ogilvie Mountains, bare and rocky apart from a sparse growth of conifers, undergrowth, mosses and lichens on their southern slopes. This is the start of Dempster Highway (left). – Lichen on the tundra in the Barrenlands (bottom).

"You could say we attracted Eskimos from the Arctic islands by giving them refrigerators. Today we act according to the principle that they themselves must work for the money they want to spend. The government mustn't say it, but the intention is for them to abandon their ethnic and cultural uniqueness – become Canadians and get lost."

Other white people besides the military and missionaries came to the north after oil was discovered in the Mackenzie valley in 1920 and extensive iron ore deposits in Labrador in 1945. Often these prospectors wore broad metal rings on their oversized braces that looked like the frame of a crinoline; they were in fact electromagnetometers for tracking down mineral deposits in the earth. A few examples show how successful they were.

In Pine Point Mines on Great Slave Lake, they established the world's highest-yielding tin and lead mines. "At the beginning we had no concentrators and shipped the ore in its raw state. It was such high quality that the company recovered their investment of 23 million dollars with the profits from a single year's production," recounted engineer Pat MacIlroy on the site. And in Whitehorse on the Yukon, the President of the local Chamber of Commerce remarked, "We export more than the whole of the Gold Rush brought in using the railway built in 1900 for the Klondike gold-diggers." Today, in Fort McMurray in northern Alberta, digging machines ten stories high shovel mud that looks like coffee grounds mixed with molasses. When this mass is boiled at 500 degrees under steam, it yields crude oil. The total deposits in this area are estimated at around 600 billion barrels – enough on its own to secure the world's current petroleum needs for the next 100 years.

However, well over half of the eleven billion barrels in the Prudhoe Bay field off the north coast of Alaska, North America's richest oilfield, have already been pumped along the Trans-Alaska Pipeline to the port

Garden idyll in the old quarter of Yellowknife, capital of the Northwest Territories (top). – Glowing salt plains in the sub-Arctic Wood Buffalo National Park (right).

of Valdez on the southern coast – the name a reminder of the greatest ecological disaster the Arctic north has ever experienced.

In March 1989, the supertanker Exxon Valdez ran onto a reef 30 miles off the coast and leaked over 42,000 tons of crude oil into the sea – as yet completely free of pollution. Fish stocks have still not recovered even today, and marine mammals such as the sea-otters and orcas in Prince William Sound show increased levels of mortality and infertility. In the drilling area of Prudhoe Bay, the world's largest assembly of engine-powered drilling pumps expels roughly as much nitrogen oxide into the atmosphere as the entire city of Delaware. One year after the USA had discovered oil in the Beaufort Sea, in 1970, the Canadian government wisely passed the Canadian Arctic Waters Pollution Prevention Act. To increase its effect, Canada extended its territorial waters from 3 to 12 nautical miles from the coast – an act which the USA still refuses to recognize today, since the Northwest Passage then passes through Canadian nautical territory, while the USA continues to claim the route as international waters in order to be able to dive between the Arctic islands in its atomic submarines without requiring the approval of another authority. Canada has foregone exploration of its own oil reserves in the Beaufort Sea, probably for reasons of cost.

Recently, the Ottawa government invited two Inuit organizations (one for the western and one for the eastern part of the Canadian Arctic) to play a central role in planning decisions for the exploitation and protection of the sensitive natural environment in the region. In 1984 the government established the 10,000-square-kilometer (4,000-square-mile) Northern Yukon National Park along the Alaskan border, to protect the environment of the world's largest herds of caribou and the Inuit people who live from them. Two years previously, all inhabitants of the Northwest Territories had taken part in a referendum and reached a decision that would resonate into the future: with effect from April 1, 1999, the Inuit were to have their own autonomous country, including all rights to land and natural resources. The new province extends from the tree line to the islands of the High Arctic, encompassing almost one-quarter of Canada's entire area. The Inuit proudly name it Nunavut, "our country". Over two million square kilometers (770,000 square miles) in area, it houses almost 30 widely scattered communities and a total of no more than 28,000 people. 85 percent of them are Inuit, and the majority of the remainder are known as temporary citizens, primarily assembly workers in the mines, generally new immigrants from many different countries, and staff of the social and national institutions. It is clear that the experiment of entrusting the establishment of an infrastructure in line with today's

A paradise for animals: musk oxen in the Barrenlands (left). – A Barren-Ground caribou (top). – A hungry brown bear catches himself a tasty supper of fish (bottom).

standards and requirements to a people who two or three generations ago were exclusively nomadic subsistence hunters living in a moneyless society is an extremely difficult task with an uncertain outcome, despite the high subsidies from Ottawa. A glance at the remaining Northwest Territories and neighboring Yukon Territory shows immediately that Nunavut still lacks the essential pre-

On the Alaska Highway at Haines Junction (left). – The truck drives mile after mile through the isolation, up Dempster Highway from Dawson City to Inuvik on the Mackenzie River delta: here at Cornwall River (bottom).

requisites for improved development. Apart from the rivers themselves, the other two territories have major routes such as the Mackenzie or Yellowknife Highway, and even routes which have grown famous such as Alaska or Dempster Highway. Nunavut, on the other hand, is a pathless tundra where the only mode of transport is sled or aircraft. Only a few dedicated tourists are likely to decide to visit the Arctic under winter conditions. However, the summer thaw transforms broad tracts of the permafrost ground into extensive mosquito-ridden swamps. Yet in the few short months of the continuous midnight sun, the country unfolds a breathtaking beauty and diversity. On Banks Island to the north of the 70th latitude, over 170 varieties of plant have been counted. Vast herds of caribou sweep across the lichen-strewn tundra; foxes, bears and wolves prowl on their search for food, and migratory birds arrive in great flocks to breed on the sheltered grassy islands of the floodplain. In the Yukon and the catchment area of the Mackenzie, this advanced edge of development has been exploited since the days of the Gold Rush, to push forward excavation of the natural resources and establish settlements at the crossroads that may develop into regional centers such as Whitehorse, capital of the Yukon Territory, where almost two-thirds of the entire population of the Territory now live.

The benefits to nature when it is not trampled by hordes of people could be seen in Nahanni National Park on the borders of the Yukon and Northwest Territories – if it were possible to get there.

park, the first natural site ever to be accepted by UNESCO for its World Heritage Site list, you need either the charter fee for a small aircraft, or stamina and experience as a canoeist. The Slavey Indians, who hunted and fished here, kept this unique treasure concealed from the white people for many years. And who could blame them? Nature cannot bear too much humanity.

However, this is not easy. At one time, around 2,000 people attempted it together; that was the fall of 1897, when the Gold Rush hit the Klondike. From Fort Simpson on the Mackenzie, they battled their way up Liard River in laden canoes, and anyone who succeeded in getting further finally succumbed to the Nahanni rapids and the encroaching Arctic winter. Place names such as Deadman Valley or Headless Range give clues about the fate of the prospectors. Fort Simpson is still the starting-point for an exploration trip to Nahanni Valley, and there is still no road. To reach this national

Camping at Kluane Lake in the Yukon (top). – The famous "signpost forest" of Watson Lake is still growing; many tourists leave their visiting cards here. The forest was begun in 1942 by a homesick construction worker. There are now over 30,000 signs here at the crossroads of Alaska Highway and Campbell Highway (left).

To find their way in the expanses of the north – as here in Sambaa Deh Falls Territorial Park in the Northwest Territories – the Inuit set up "inukshuk", stone figures that mark the paths. – Alexandra Falls in Twin Falls Gorge Territorial Park (right).

HUNTERS OF THE NORTH
THE INUIT

After catching diseases from a white ship's crew, the last Sadlermiut people died in 1902 on Southampton Island in the northern Hudson Bay. According to what is known about these people, they had previously lived without any contact to modern civilization, with a way of life akin to Stone Age hunters, and were probably the last representatives of the Neolithic Dorset Inuit.

over 150 stone foundations of summer dwellings that carbon dating revealed had been inhabited up to 850 B.C. were identified by archeologists on the Bache peninsula, at the border of what is known as a polynya, an area in the Arctic pack ice which remains free from ice thanks to its special microclimate and

The first precursors of the Dorset culture (simply named Pre-Dorset, for want of any individual designation, after Cape Dorset (Kinngait), an archeological site on Baffin Island) first emerged around 4,000 years ago on this side of the Bering Strait in the Canadian Arctic. Their immediate descendants, the Dorset people, established the most northerly prehistoric settlement known to us, on the 79th latitude on Ellesmere Island in the High Arctic. A total of

warm ocean currents. It is naturally attractive for marine mammals which need to surface to breathe – and which are the preferred prey of the Inuit hunters. While the Pre-Dorset people left only flint blades up to eight centimeters (3 inches) long, the Dorset people who followed from the 7th century developed igloos and harpoons with toggle heads, and carved beautifully detailed small figures of the animals they hunted from ivory and bone, wearing them as amulets or using them for hunting magic and other animist rites. The figures

Fishing plays the greatest role in the lives of the Inuit people: Inuit in a motor-boat on the Beaufort Sea near Paulatuk, Northwest Territories (left). The name refers to the coal reserves in nearby Tuktut Nogait National Park. Ice fishing on Padlee Lake, Baffin Island, in Nunavut (top center). "Nunavut", meaning "our land" in Inuktitut, has been under the autonomous rule of the Inuit themselves since 1999. – Inuk with salmon trout on a Ski-doo sled at Paulatuk (bottom center). Twin-otter aircraft in Paulatuk (right-hand page, top). Loasie Kooneeliusie hunting seal in Pangnirtung Fjord, Baffin Island (right-hand page, bottom).

the connection between all living things. The animism of the Inuit is founded in the belief that everything in nature has a soul and a spirit, and thus all living creatures are related. An animal that permits itself to be hunted, they assumed would also "permit" the hunter to kill it. It sacrificed itself willingly to serve as food for humans.

Sculptures of the great northern diver are common, and Jean Malaurie, certainly one of the greatest experts on the Inuit, pointed out that the North American loon (or diver) frequently accompanies the souls into the kingdom of the dead in the myths and legends of many autochthonous peoples. We know today that evolutionarily speaking, the divers are an ancient species that has remained unchanged for millions of years, and their primeval cry still sends a shiver down our spine. In the 10th century, the settlement on Ellesmere Island

include expressive carvings of polar bears in thumbnail size. Humanoid figures probably represent the embodiments of evil spirits which the shamans attempted to banish. (In some regions, the Inuit of today still carve these "tupilaks" from the tusks of orcas.)

Despite the naturalism, many animals feature a carving of their skeleton, probably a reference to the transition between life and death or to the soul of the animal as a spirit. Violating the spirit of the animals that permitted humans to hunt and eat them would have meant denying

was taken over by a new culture, and the Dorset Inuit vanished relatively rapidly after the year 1000.

The new arrivals had also come over the Bering Strait from Siberia, and had even brought the art of pottery with them, although this was soon forgotten owing to the lack of wood to fire kilns. These Thule Eskimos, however, were superior to their forefathers in one respect: they brought dog sleds and larger boats suitable for whaling. These Thule Eskimos were the forerunners of today's Inuit. Their handicrafts formed a uniform style extending around the Polar ice cap, and, via the ice off Ellesmere Island, also reached as far as the last stage of their journey from west to east: Greenland, where they forced the Vikings coming from Iceland into the south.

In 1980, remains of an iron chain-mail shirt and of woven woolen cloth from the mid-13th century were discovered near the Inuit settlement on Ellesmere Island. The question is how these items of the European Nordic peoples came to be here.

We owe Knud Johan Rasmussen much of our knowledge of the culture and way of life of the

Inuit. Born in 1879 in Greenland as the son of a Danish missionary and an indigenous woman, he learnt Danish at school, but was driving his own dog team at the age of eight, and learnt hunting and many survival techniques from his Inuit relatives. His father later sent him to university in Copenhagen, but at the age of 23 he signed up as an interpreter for a Danish expedition through Greenland, and in 1910 was a founder member of the Arctic research station of Thule in Northern Greenland, taking part in expeditions researching the Arctic and the life of the Inuit from this base station. His most important mission was the fifth, which began in June 1921 and lasted over four years. On this, Rasmussen collected the tales and legends of the Eskimos, translating them himself, while the scientists accompanying him gathered data on Arctic zoology, geology and mineralogy. The expedition traveled through the Inuit's entire territory, from Greenland to the Canadian Arctic and beyond the Pacific, and Rasmussen became known as the first person to conquer the Northwest Passage by dog sled. On December 21, 1933, Knud Rasmussen died on his eighth Arctic exhibition.

Snowstorm in Paulatuk (left-hand page, top). – Abraham Pijamini from Grise Fjord (Ausuittuq) on Ellesmere Island (right-hand page, bottom left). – Two Inuit, photo from 1933 (right-hand page, bottom right). – "Dancing Shaman with Drum", sculpture in dark green soapstone (center, bottom left). – "Woman with Bear", sculpture (center, bottom right). – Stone carving "Spirit", shaman with animal mask (center, bottom right). – Inuit women (top left and right). – Stone carving "Three Skin Boats, Whaling" (main picture).

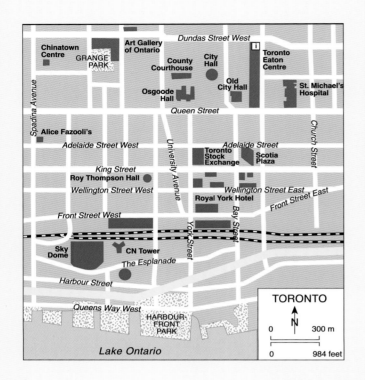

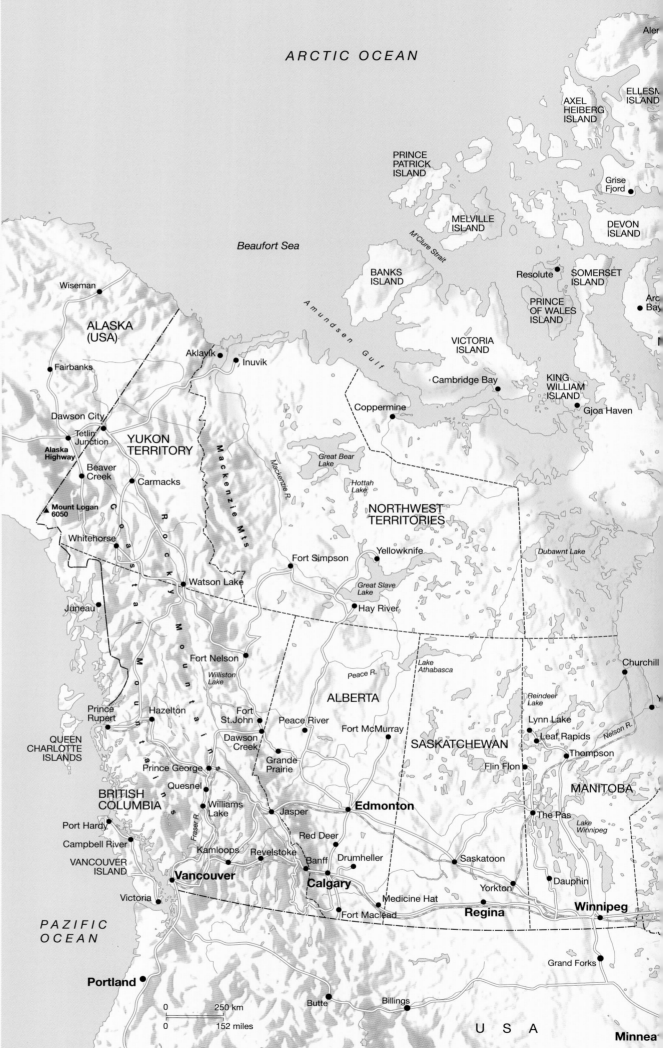

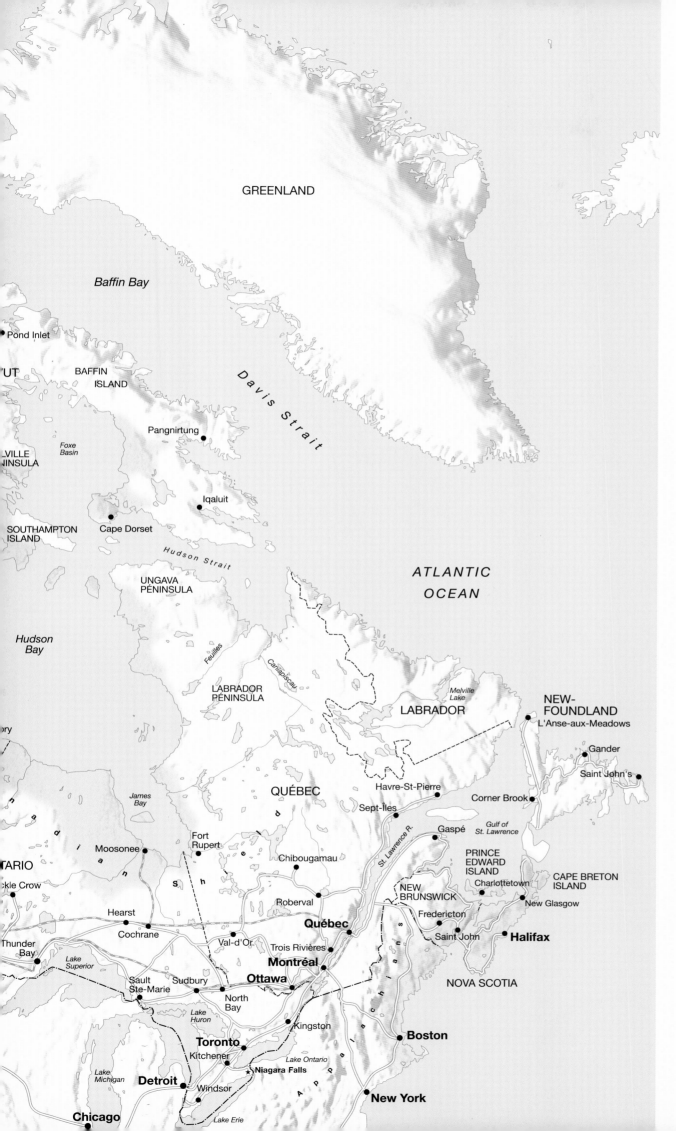

GREENLAND

Baffin Bay

Pond Inlet

'UT

BAFFIN
ISLAND

*Foxe
Basin*

VILLE
'NINSULA

Davis Strait

Pangnirtung

SOUTHAMPTON
ISLAND

Cape Dorset

Iqaluit

Hudson Strait

ATLANTIC
OCEAN

UNGAVA
PÉNINSULA

*Hudson
Bay*

ory

*James
Bay*

Feuilles

Cariapiscau

LABRADOR
PÉNINSULA

*Melville
Lake*

LABRADOR

NEW-
FOUNDLAND
L'Anse-aux-Meadows

Gander

Saint John's

QUÉBEC

Havre-St-Pierre

Corner Brook

Sept-Îles

Moosonee

Fort
Rupert

Gaspé

*Gulf of
St. Lawrence*

'kle Crow

Chibougamau

PRINCE
EDWARD
ISLAND

CAPE BRETON
ISLAND

'ARIO

Roberval

NEW
BRUNSWICK

Charlottetown

New Glasgow

Hearst

St. Lawrence R.

Fredericton

Cochrane

Val-d'Or

Québec

Saint John

Halifax

Thunder
Bay

*Lake
Superior*

Trois Rivières

Montréal

NOVA SCOTIA

Sault
Ste-Marie

Sudbury

Ottawa

North
Bay

*Lake
Huron*

Kingston

Toronto

Boston

Kitchener

Lake Ontario

Niagara Falls

*Lake
Michigan*

Detroit

Windsor

Lake Erie

New York

Chicago

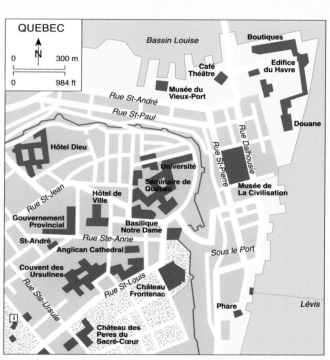

QUEBEC

N

0   300 m

0   984 ft

Bassin Louise

Boutiques

Café
Théâtre

Edifice
du Havre

Musée du
Vieux-Port

Rue St-André

Rue St-Paul

Douane

Hôtel Dieu

Rue St-Pierre

Université

Rue St-Jean

Séminaire de
Québec

Hôtel de
Ville

Rue Dalhousie

Musée de
La Civilisation

Gouvernement
Provincial

Basilique
Notre Dame

Rue Ste-Anne

St-André

Anglican Cathedral

Sous le Port

Couvent des
Ursulines

Rue St-Louis

Château
Frontenac

Phare

Lévis

Rue Ste-Ursule

Château des
Peres du
Sacré-Coeur

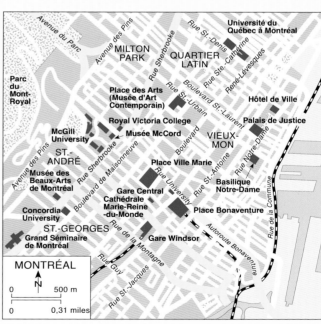

Avenue du Parc

Avenue des Pins

Rue St-Denis

Université du
Québec à Montréal

MILTON
PARK

Rue Sherbrooke

QUARTIER
LATIN

Rue Ste-Catherine

René-Lévesques

Parc
du
Mont-
Royal

Place des Arts
(Musée d'Art
Contemporain)

Boulevard St-Laurent

Hôtel de Ville

Royal Victoria College

Palais de Justice

McGill
University

Musée McCord

Boulevard

VIEUX-
MON

Rue Notre-Dame

ST.-
ANDRÉ

Avenue des Pins

Rue Sherbrooke

Place Ville Marie

Musée des
Beaux-Arts
de Montréal

Boulevard de Maisonneuve

Rue University

Basilique
Notre-Dame

Gare Central
Cathédrale
Marie-Reine
-du-Monde

Rue St-Antoine

Rue de la Commune

Concordia
University

Place Bonaventure

ST.-GEORGES

Grand Séminaire
de Montréal

Gare Windsor

Autoroute Bonaventure

Rue de la Montagne

Rue Guy

Rue St-Jacques

MONTRÉAL

N

0   500 m

0   0,31 miles

Index

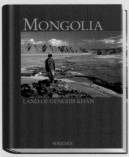
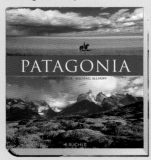
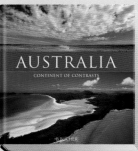

The photographer

Christian Heeb born in 1962, is one of the world's most successful travel photographers. His photos have been published in more than 90 books, countless calendars, and in well-known European magazines such as Animan and Grands Reportages. In 2007 Bucher Publishing has also published his volumes about Mexico and Morocco. Heeb lives on a ranch in Bend, Oregon. He is a member of the Cologne-based agency laif and the Paris agency Hémisphères. His photographs are published and exhibited internationally.
See www.heebphoto.com

The author

Karl-Ludwig Wetzig, born in 1956, is a freelance author and translator whose love of Nordic lands has been a life-long affair, and whose passion for the north includes Canada. He has published numerous illustrated travel books on topics as diverse as Cambodia and Iceland. He is also publishing articles about his travels from Greenland to South-East Asia in well-known magazines such as "Tours", "Nordis", "Mare", "Frankfurter Rundschau" and "Lettre International".

Cover photos:
Front: Peyto Peak Towers, literally towering above the lake of the same name. (Christian Heeb)
page 1: Hopewell Rocks in the Bay of Fundy. (Christian Heeb)

page 210/211: Lighthouse, Cape Spear National Historic Site, Newfoundland. (Christian Heeb)

Credits

Archiv für Kunst und Geschichte, Berlin: p. 85 r., 112 r.b., 150/151, 194 l. c., 209;
Bildarchiv Preußischer Kulturbesitz, Berlin: p. 84/85, 84 l., 85 b., 195 r.t. (2), 208 c.;
Bilderberg / Peter Arnold / Charles Russel, Hamburg: p. 180;
Oliver Bolch, Maria Enzersdorf: p. 164 t.;
Canada Science and Technology Museum, Ottawa: p. 103 r.c., 126/127;
Corbis: p. 86 l. (Lowell Georgia), 103 r.t. (Hulton Deutsch Collection), 151 r.t., 151 r.c.;
Glenbow Archives, Calgary: p. 87 l.t. und r.t., 102 l., 112 c., 126 l., 126 b., 127 b., 127 r.t., 150 l., 151 l.c. and b.;
Hansmann – Kulturgeschichtliches Bildarchiv, Munich: p. 208/209, 208 b., 209 l.b. (2);
Interfoto, Munich: p. 20 c., 21 b., 86/87;
Helga Lade, Frankfurt: p. 102/103;
Laif, Cologne: p. 103 b. (Amme), 181 b.c. l. and r. (Harscher), 181 b.l. und t.r. (Specht);
LOOK, München: p. 56/57 und 57 b. (2) (Widmann), 58 b. und 59 t. (Schwermer);
Mary Evans Picture Library, London: p. 56 l., 58 l., 86 b., 87 r.c., 113 r.b.;
Okapia, Frankfurt: p. 181 r.c. (Wiede) und r.b. (McDonald);
Karl-Heinz Raach, Freiburg: p. 182 b. (3), 184/185, 185 b.l. und b.C., 192/193, 204/205, 206/207, 206 l., 207 b., 207 r.t., 207 r.c., 208 (2);
Roger Viollet, Paris: p. 44/45, 45 r.t. und l.b.;
Sammlung Dietmar Siegert, Munich: p. 59 b.;
Süddeutscher Bilderdienst, Munich: p. 21 r.c.;
Hanna Wagner, Wörth: p. 50 t.;
Wolfgang R. Weber, Darmstadt: p 4/5, 14, 24 (2);
Wolfgang R. Weber, Darmstadt / Yukon Archives: p. 194/195, 194 t., 195 l.c., 195 r.c

All other photographs were taken by Christian Heeb.

We would like to thank all the copyright owners and publishers for their printing permissions. Although we made every effort, we were unable to identify every single one of the copyright owners. We would kindly ask them to contact C.J. Bucher Publishing.

This work has been carefully researched by the author and kept up to date as well as checked by the publisher for coherence. However, the publishing house can assume no liability for the accuracy of the data contained herein.
We are always grateful for suggestions and advice. Please send your comments to:
C.J. Bucher Publishing,
Product Management
Innsbrucker Ring 15
81673 Munich
Germany
E-mail:
editorial@bucher-publishing.com
Homepage:
www.bucher-publishing.com

Translation: Alison Moffat-McLynn, Munich, Germany
Proof-reading: Toby Skingsley, Munich, Germany
Graphic design: Werner Poll, Munich, Germany, revised by Agnes Meyer-Wilmes, Munich, Germany
Cartography: Astrid Fischer-Leitl, Munich, Germany

Product management for the German edition: Joachim Hellmuth
Product management for the English edition: Dr. Birgit Kneip
Production: Bettina Schippel
Repro: Repro Ludwig, Zell am See, Austria
Printed in Italy by Printer Trento

ISBN 987-3-7658-1631-4